THE LOGIC OF THE FAITH

THE
LOGIC OF THE FAITH

HENRI BOUILLARD, S.J.

SHEED AND WARD : NEW YORK

Originally published as
Logique de la Foi
by Editions Aubier, Paris

Nihil obstat: Michael Bertramus Crowe
Censor Theol. Deput.
Imprimi potest: ✠Ioannes Carolus
Archiep. Dublinen.
Hiberniae Primas

Dublini, die 20a Januarii, anno 1967.

Library of Congress Catalog Card Number 67-18012

Manufactured in the United States of America

CONTENTS

PART THREE

PHILOSOPHICAL APPROACHES

PREFACE

"All philosophizing is inspired by the same primitive, persistent idea and intention; a single word, no doubt, could contain them, yet all the books in the world would not exhaust what they contain." This remark of Maurice Blondel's strikes us as being of very general application. By the intellectual effort a writer chooses to put into a philosophical, theological or other similar work, he can make it, in certain respects at least, peculiarly his own. In any event, Blondel's remark put an end to any scruples we may have had when some friends of ours encouraged us to bring together, in one volume, various papers on religious philosophy, Christian apologetics or fundamental theology, which first saw the light at intervals over a period of fifteen years or so. The mutual relation of the papers and articles assembled here may not, at first glance, be immediately obvious. They were made to order—if I may say so—each for a special purpose, and each for insertion in a different context. None the less, the same idea and intention actuate them all, and that is to bring out the underlying correspondence between the logic of human existence and the call of the Christian mystery, and, by so doing, to uncover the rational pattern of the process that leads to acceptance of the Christian faith—in short, to reveal the logic of that faith.

Our intention will be most apparent in the first chapter. Its object is to define the meaning of apologetics in terms of the real nature of the certitude of faith, due regard being had to the tendency of contemporary man to think he is living under the Nietzschean sign: "God is dead!" Apologetics, to our mind, is not simply a defence of religion against those who attack it. It is a positive activity, a working-out of the logic of the movement of men's minds towards the faith. It is at once a philosophy of Christianity and a fundamental theology. The chapter on the liberty of the Christian demonstrates that, in fact, the exigencies of Christian morals are in line with the nature of human behaviour and so promote the logic of liberty.

These chapters are followed by a series of dialogues with different forms of Protestant thought. There is a dialogue with Kierkegaard on the proper character of faith and the conditions governing the process of "becoming a Christian". There are dialogues with Barth and Bultmann on the relation of "natural theology" to knowledge of the faith; and another dialogue with Bultmann on the existential interpretation, and the de-mythologization, of the New Testament. These dialogues make no attempt to lay down minimal conditions for communion in one single and only Church. In this particular sense they have no ecumenical character. They aim, however, at enlarging the ecumenical idea and giving it a contemporary and realistic turn. Theologians of different Christian denominations have to take one another seriously even when they disagree, each side trying to appreciate what is well-grounded and of consequence in the points made by the other side, so that all may arrive together at a better understanding of the gospel. By adopting this attitude, it seemed to us that we could learn valuable lessons or at least glean suggestions, from the works of thinkers and theologians as far apart as Kierkegaard, Barth and Bultmann, at the same time bringing out the intrinsic reasons that limit our concurrence in their opinions. Though retaining their idea of faith as an existential decision when confronted with Christ, the one and only source of revelation, we have felt it necessary to stress more strongly than they how deeply rooted this faith is in the logic of human existence.

To analyse the deep-rootedness of faith, it is extremely useful to know the views of the philosophers who have given much thought to it. Of these we have chosen two: Gabriel Marcel and Maurice Blondel. The first will tell us how concrete approaches to the ontological mystery can pave the way for acceptance of the Christian message; the second, how the logic of action even meets Christianity half-way and, without going so far as to declare the faith imperative, is led inevitably to pose the religious problem in Christian terms. There is no question, be it understood, of taking the views of these philosophers as absolute norms. Besides, they differ appreciably from each other. Both, however, have thrown light on essential points and can, therefore, be of help to those engaged in the same line of inquiry.

These, then, are the three parts of our book. And, as we have already indicated, the perspective within which its several elements are unified is our concern to bring out as best we can the logic of the Christian faith.

Before we go any farther we must hasten to remove any doubts about what we have just said, by being a little more explicit. By logic of the faith we mean, of course, the logic of free adherence to the Christian mystery. It lies in the correspondence between the gospel message and the logic of human existence, this correspondence being both perceived and freely acknowledged. But it also obviously implies that the transcendence of the divinely revealed mystery and its meaning for us must be safeguarded at all costs. Therefore, the logic of the faith is not reducible to the logic of human existence; indeed its full content is not revealed until one freely surrenders to it.

In fact, as the philosophers we shall consult later in this book will confirm, no analysis of human existence could conclude as to the necessity of the incarnation or discover the contents of the Christian message. The spontaneous manifestation of God in history, in the person of Christ, is a contingent, an absolutely unique, event. Only by obedient adherence to the historical gospel message can we get to know its mystery and learn to live by it. Even when reflection has helped us to discern the mystery of being or to feel the spell of the "one thing necessary" (which is God), we should remember Blondel's words: "Apart from the drama—the divine drama—being enacted in every man's conscience, the souls of true believers, from the very first, become aware of a new mystery of grace that revelation alone can unveil, and then only in part."[1] In the words of St Paul: ". . . we impart a secret and hidden wisdom of God, which God decreed before the ages for our glorification . . . it is written, What no eye has seen, nor ear heard, nor the heart of man conceived, what God has prepared for those who love him."[2] Access to this divine wisdom is to be had only through faith in Christ and by the light of the holy Spirit.

This heavenly wisdom which, St Paul observed, was folly in the eyes of the "world", could surely never look utterly foreign to the eyes of man, who, after all, is created to God's image. Indeed, the apostle, in another passage, appealed to a vision vouchsafed to him by God, in order to make his hearers understand that the gospel message concerned them. If it is

[1] M. Blondel, *Lettre sur l'Apologétique* in *Les premiers écrits de Maurice Blondel* II, Paris 1956, 88–89.
[2] I *Cor.* 2:7, 9.

true that Christ has a decisive importance for all men, then Christ's coming must respond to something congenital in man's make-up which is open to the supernatural and gives rise to a vague expectancy in the human heart. Otherwise we should not be able to discern that Christ is the Word of God for us. The logic of human existence must allow man's supernatural orientation to be perceived, be it ever so dimly, and must give some indication of the method by which rational adherence to the divine revelation can be effected. Doubtless, only those already acquainted with the Christian reality will be able to discern that method by themselves. At any rate, they will not have to create it; they will find it by reflecting upon man's being. They will find, too, that the logic of existence, though it does not convey the actual sense of the gospel message, constitutes the dawn phase of its disclosure. And so they will see the logic of faith as the logic of rational adherence to the Christian mystery.

But all these subtleties, which we can only mention here, will be explained in the pages that follow. Of course, a book like this could never manage to say everything. Indeed, it can only be a rough draft for an inquiry we hope to pursue and develop in greater depth some day, in a more homogeneous work. Perhaps, however, the insights it provides will be of some service to those who are charged with the task of presenting the gospel message to the people of our time. Perhaps, also, they will fortify the faith of a few Christians by shedding more light on it, or even help some non-believers to see that Christianity not only has meaning, but has meaning for them.

THE LOGIC OF THE FAITH

PART ONE

Faith, Life and Liberty

I

THE NATURE OF APOLOGETICS

1. *Definition and function*

Christian apologetics, in the classical sense, is the theoretical and methodical exposition of the reasons for believing in Christianity. It is not to be confused with the psychology of conversion; it does not describe the diverse routes taken by souls on their way to the Christian fold; its proper object is to state the reasons`for Christian belief. These it sets out in the form of a general theory in which all essential questions are systematically reviewed and the findings given as universal a bearing as possible.

Christian apologetics differs, therefore, from the art of the apostolate, which consists in placing before certain individuals or groups considerations likely to appeal to them, recognizing and resolving any difficulties, and suggesting to them the attitude of mind that will enable them to see things in a clearer light. The apostle's art, it may be assumed, is acquired by actual experience rather than academic teaching. On the other hand, what can be taught is the theory of the credibility of Christianity, the rational justification of the act of faith.

Now the rational justification of faith should, of its very nature, be of value to every human soul, Christian or not. True, Maurice Blondel insisted that its business was "to say something that will carry weight with those who do not believe". We should not, however, take this to mean that our theoretical exposition of the reasons for our belief is intended solely for the conversion of non-believers. It is also of concern to those who believe, for it brings out one of the essential characteristics, one of the permanent conditions, of faith. And that is the conviction that not only is the Christian faith reasonable but—what is far more—that it is compelling, imperative. The credibility of Christianity always goes hand in hand with the Christian faith—not that the Christian is continually preoccupied with it, but in the sense that it is always available for recall when he or others may need it.

The process of reasoning whereby one becomes satisfied that Christianity is credible and becomes convinced that one not only *can* believe but *must* believe, is not by any means peculiar to the non-believer in course of conversion. It can also take place in the mind of the believer, without any suggestion that his mind has been troubled by pre-existing doubts. A sound exposition of the reasons for the faith that is in him offers the committed Christian a means of re-affirming his faith. It rids him of that inferiority complex which so many Christians feel when confronted by non-believers. It enables him to take his stand solidly and surely in an atheistic environment. More important still, it gives him a better understanding of his faith, because it brings him back to its secure foundations. From this point of view, indeed, apologetics would be better described as fundamental theology. Later on, I shall have occasion to say more about this. For the moment I would point out that apologetics would justify its existence even if it proved completely ineffectual in influencing non-believers.

But is it true, as some allege, that apologetics never succeeds in converting anybody? Admittedly, some books on Christian apologetics are not very helpful. They are so unconvincing that even believers find them unsatisfactory. They are superficial and burke the real problems; they lack method and handle their material so inadequately that the conclusions which emerge are quite incapable of satisfying an exacting mind.

On the other hand, there are also treatises on apologetics that can well be classified as outstanding; these continue to exert a profound influence. If we take inspiration and example from them we may hope that what we say will carry weight with non-believers.

Let us be very clear, however, as to how, and within what limits, apologetics can have any efficacy at all. A neurotic patient needs something more for his cure than a course of reading in psychiatry. No more does the study of a treatise on Christian apologetics suffice to bring men to Christ. By and large, the theoretical treatise only indicates in a general way an attitude of mind for adoption. It does not inevitably bring about the act by which this attitude is effectively adopted. That is not to say it is of no use; without the indications given by it, the reader would not know the road to take.

I have used the word "attitude". That is the right word, seeing that what is in question is the Christian faith. For the faith is not just the acceptance of a certain number of dogmas. It is the movement of the soul towards God, personal adherence to Christ, willingness to live as a Christian in the bosom of the Church. The intellectual assent that precedes conversion is itself an entirely voluntary act, an act of perfectly free choice; it is not necessarily compelled by the force of any argument.

No reason for believing dispenses with the act of believing. All apologetics, like all preaching, here meets the limit of its efficacy. But if it is true that faith is in accordance with reason, then we cannot believe without reason. And that is where apologetics comes into its own.

2. *The sure basis of our faith*

To understand more exactly the role and range of apologetics, we must call to mind the grounds on which our conviction of the truth of our faith is based. The First Vatican Council, after surveying the corpus of traditional doctrine, declared that we believe, not because we should ever be able to apprehend the intrinsic truth of the Christian message by the light of our natural reason, but because of the authority of God who reveals it. The question, therefore, is how we can be certain that the Christian message is God's revelation?

Can the fact of revelation be proved by historical arguments? If it is true that God reveals himself through the mediation of certain historical personages, undoubtedly historical knowledge of those personages plays a part in assuring us of the truth of our faith. But it is no less clear that this alone is not a sufficient basis on which to build our belief. What is involved here is not the question of knowing whether a historical demonstration supplies real evidence, or just a probability, or—more often than not—a discreet conviction. For—and let us make no mistake about it— the divine reality as such is not dependent on the mere opinion of a historian.

God is God. He is the Totally Other, incommensurable with intramundane realities. He dwells in an inaccessible light. We cannot know him, then, except through himself. If we discern him in the world about us and in our own souls, it is because he chooses to manifest himself there. If we perceive him in certain historical figures, it is because he chose to reveal himself through them. And we have no means of knowing that he really and truly reveals himself except his own revelation.

How does that revelation manage to make itself felt, we are bound to ask? How does it impose itself on us, on each of us, penetrating to the very core of our spiritual being? We can only answer that it brings conviction with it. We have the certitude that God reveals himself from the very fact that he does reveal himself to us, to each of us believers.

Revelation, in fact, does not simply consist of the objective reality of Christ and the Church, or of the objective tenor of the Christian message. There is no revelation independent of the souls that receive it. A revelation that was not received by anyone would be a misnomer. Revelation is always made to someone. Let us recall Christ's words to Peter after Peter's avowal at Caesarea: "Blessed are you, Simon Bar-Jona! For flesh and blood has not revealed this to you, but my Father who is in heaven" (*Matt.*. 16:17). It was the heavenly Father who revealed the supernatural character of Jesus to the prince of the apostles. It is God himself who is the revealer, and he reveals himself to the believer in the very act of faith which he determines and evokes.

In theological teaching this idea is commonly presented in a somewhat different form. The determining factor in believing is described as the light of grace, as the holy Spirit shedding his light upon our souls and drawing them to God—the *instinctus interior Dei invitantis.* But this is sometimes interpreted too imaginatively, as if man were faced with a revelation independent of all perception, to discern and accept which he would be favoured with a supernatural light, which would let him see the revelation, and a supernatural impulse which would urge or draw him towards it. In reality there is no objective revelation beyond that which is apprehended by human souls, and the divine light in the soul is nothing other than that of the revelation received. The Word that God pronounces in Jesus Christ reaches the believer's soul through the medium of the holy Spirit. And the light of faith is this very Word in so far as it is apprehended by the believer.

God reveals himself to each of us in the heart of the act of faith which he determines and evokes. Our consciousness of this revelation has the quality of a direct, personal intuition; it is an intimate experience, a supernatural perception analogous to mystical knowledge. Today this is admitted by many theologians. And it is this experience of God that constitutes the sure basis of our faith.[1]

But we should beware of illuminism. I have said that the divine revelation brings conviction with it and that our certitude in its regard comes from our direct apprehension of it. By this I mean that it imposes itself upon us *per se* in the course of an experience personal to each of us. We must stress, however, no less strongly, that God always reveals himself through an intermediate agency, under the sign and veil of things distinct from him; we always know him in an indirect way, through signs.

Because God is infinite and we are infinitely beneath him, we cannot apprehend him in himself; we can only know him through his works. The natural knowledge that we can have of him consists of what we can discern of his manifestation of himself in the world and in the human soul. Knowledge of God by faith consists in recognizing him in the historical signs of his actual revelation. Whoever says revelation says manifestation by signs. By signs we mean not alone miracles of the physical or moral order but the totality of divine action that

---

[1]Cf. Roger Aubert, *Le Problème de l'acte de foi* (*3e edition*), Louvain 1958, 721-34: "La perception surnaturelle du motif de foi". Also *ibid*, 587-644.

constitutes the history of salvation, the totality of creatures that God has selected and sanctified so that they may be the signs of his presence and the instruments of his action, in the history of mankind. The sign of signs is the human reality of Jesus Christ.

But the attestation of God in Jesus has been the object of both expectation and commemoration. The Jews, whose Messiah he was, had looked forward to his coming, while the Church, inaugurated by the faith and preaching of the apostles, has never ceased to commemorate him. And so we may say that God's attestation in Jesus—the period during which the signs of Christian revelation are manifest—stretches, in unbroken continuity, back into the history of the people of Israel and forward into the history of the Church. It is always through those signs, and therefore indirectly, that the believer encounters the divine revelation.

But note that these signs are not the middle term in a line of reasoning that would inevitably lead to the conclusion that God has actually revealed himself. They are the place or juncture in which we experience, the transparency (so to speak) in which we perceive, the revelation God is making to us. The point at which they mediate is the point of immediate contact between God as he reveals himself and the surge of faith that rises to meet him in the revelation. We do not reason from the signs to the revelation; we read the revelation in the signs.

But while we read the revelation in the signs, our perception of it is none the less obscure. Indeed the historical personages who bear witness to God screen him also from our sight. In order to reveal himself, God abases himself. Even the humanity of Christ implies an abasement of God and hides his real being. And how much more does it hide the human reality of the Church which can present such an equivocal aspect to the non-believer! In all the things that God uses as signs in revealing himself, he veils himself even as he reveals himself. One can remain blind to his revelation. One can even be scandalized at having to acknowledge the Absolute in a human—all too human—reality. We are sure, perhaps, that we have him in our grasp at last, only to find that he has again eluded us. In the words of St Thomas Aquinas: "The revelation made to us in this life does not tell us what God is, and so our union with him is like union with an unknown Being".[2] In other words, God, even in revealing himself, remains a mystery, and it is as a mystery that he discloses himself to the believer.

Revelation, then, does not lend itself to being attested as an evident fact; we can only recognize it by agreeing to regard it as the mystery that it is. In a very real sense I perceive God revealing himself in a way that does not dispense me from believing he is revealing himself. To discern the reality of the revelation and to discern the duty to believe in it, are, therefore, both one. Through the signs I apprehend the revelation as *credendum*. The act by which I apprehend it is an act of submission and the experience is an act of obedience.

Because one can fail to understand the signs of revelation and because, in fact, many do not understand them, it will be well to inquire at this stage what conditions need to be fulfilled in order that the signs may be understood.

First, we may remark that the signs would have no meaning for anyone if the mystery they were supposed to make known had no intrinsic relation to human existence. But, as it happens, their purpose is to impress on us that communion with God is our supernatural end, and this, according to patristic and medieval tradition, revived in our own day, is the object of an immanent human desire. This means that Christ and the Church offer us communion with the living God as the answer

---

[2] *S. theol.*, Ia, q. 12, a. 13, ad 1.

to the question of the meaning of human existence. We can, indeed, read God's revelation in the signs to the precise extent of our capacity to read in them also the revelation of the meaning of human existence.

Now what are the conditions that enable us to understand the signs in this sense? The message which the signs bear stipulates that we must render ourselves receptive to communion in the divine life. If we would accept that life we must agree to love it more than our own natural pleasure, and, above all, to renounce all hankering after self-sufficiency in the finite field of our own activity. Anyone who would pretend to self-sufficiency in his finiteness could only reject the notions of supernatural life and revelation. For such a person, consequently, the signs of revelation would not be signs at all but either disconcerting, or else quite unimportant, facts. To anyone who has felt the yearning for the infinite but lacks the courage to accept the self-sacrifice demanded, revelation, though he might long for it, is not for him. Nor do the signs convey anything to him, because to understand them would be to apprehend revelation. But when a man has come to understand that the absolute to which he and all mankind aspire is only to be found in the death of the individual to himself; when he is ready to practise the self-abnegation that will lay him open to God's action, then the renunciation and submission imposed by Christianity will actually appear to him as a sign of its truth. He would have none of a God who would not make such demands of him. Because he is ready to welcome communion with God, he understands the signs by which it is mediated.

One, therefore, only discerns the truth of Christianity by adopting a religious attitude of mind. Such an attitude, however, is oriented in the opposite direction to that of a certain natural human bent, and so it can be adopted and maintained only by a free effort of the will. Thus it transpires that the truth of Christianity can only be discerned if one freely chooses to discern it.

We must be more precise. The religious attitude in question is not any attitude whatever. It is a Christian attitude, and that is so even if the person who adopts it is not yet fully converted; for it is an attitude that is already within the ambit of the Christian faith. In the case of a professing Christian such an attitude shows the faith itself in operation. And with that we reach the point in our reasoning where we find that the truth of Christianity is discernible only when viewed in the attitude of faith. And the firmer and fuller this attitude, the more discernible that truth will be.

But are we not guilty of reasoning in a vicious circle if we say that intellectual perception is actually conditioned by the very attitude it sets out to justify? That will be the view only of those who harbour the delusion that knowledge and liberty, intellect and will, category and attitude, are pairs of unrelated terms. In reality each term of each pair is always conditioned by its partner. We find this confirmed whenever we delve deeply enough into the works of the human intellect. Scientists who have reflected on their work have been led to remark that to understand the theories of mathematics and physics involves a certain amount of subjective acceptance.[3] It is the same with philosophy. In his *Logique de la Philosophie*, Eric Weil, when he comes to list pure attitudes by categories, observes that the transition of one category to the next is "free", and even, in a sense, "incomprehensible".[4] That is to say, man cannot be *compelled* to go beyond the position he has

[3]See, e.g., J. L. Destouches, *Principes fondamentaux de Physique théorique*, I, 113-4.

[4]E. Weil, *Logique de la Philosophie*, Paris, 1950, 345.

taken up. Even the philosopher must be allowed full liberty to express himself!

That is all the more reason why full rein should be given to that intellectual perception whose function it is to ordain and govern man's existence. How could we ever grasp divine revelation, designed to move us to the very depths of our being, if we do not open our minds and hearts freely and lovingly to the divine invader?

It must not be thought, however, that there is nothing more to be said in dialogue with those who refuse to adopt the attitude that would allow them to see the light. If, in the realm of thought, a man cannot be compelled to shift his ground, he may be shown that he has, in fact, already done so without noticing it. An analogous possibility presents itself in the religious sphere. The non-believer can be shown how, in fact, he already accepts part at least of what he says he rejects, or he might very well be reminded that something within him sits in judgement upon, and perhaps condemns, his attitude of rejection.

3. *The apologetical treatise*

Now that we have taken a good look at the foundation on which our conviction of the truth of our faith is firmly based, and at the conditions under which that foundation can be perceived at all, we are in a better position to define the role of apologetics more precisely.

For one brief moment, perhaps, it might have seemed that we were engaged in the process of rendering any attempt at such a definition utterly futile. If it is true that my faith is founded on a personal perception of the divine revelation that compels my recognition, of what earthly use is it to discourse on the reasons for my belief? In the language of the theologians, if the motive of faith is the object of supernatural perception, what would be the relevance of any other motive or estimate of credibility or attempt at rational justification?

But we hastened to add that divine revelation is indirect, mediated by the agency of historical personages, who are its signs. There is, then, good reason for presenting these historical figures just as they appear in history.

We said that these figures conceal at the same time as they reveal, and that the revelation they bring is never so clearly perceived that we are dispensed from believing it. It is, therefore, proper that we should understand why we are under obligation to believe.

Finally, we noted that the perception of revelation and the discernment of our duty to believe were conditioned by a certain religious attitude. There is, accordingly, good reason for stating why we should adopt that religious attitude.

This brings us back to the part played by motives and estimates of credibility, and by rational justification of the faith. Where the faith is lived peaceably and without interference, and perhaps in the case of certain conversions, reasoned judgements as to the credibility of the faith, much less their explicit formulation, are scarcely to be looked for. They remain implicit in the conviction that the faith is true. But, in any event, the certitude is there, potentially, and can be formulated. Now apologetics consists precisely in making explicit in an analytical study, based on universally valid principles, the spiritual act whereby the divine revelation is discerned in historical Christianity.

In so far as such a study is analytical, it presents, in the form of a theoretical analysis, what is commonly apprehended by the individual as a synthetic perception. Inasmuch as it is of universal import, it must include some ideal, formal plan of its subject.

How are we to set about planning a work of this kind?

We have said that God's revelation would have no meaning for us if it was not also revelation of the meaning of human existence. In order to demonstrate our duty to believe, we must, therefore, show that the Christian faith is the indispensable condition for the fulfilment of our human destiny. No apologetic is of any value that does not deal somehow or other with this point. It would be useless to enumerate miracles and prodigious events if the Christian phenomenon of which they form part could not be convincingly established as the answer to the question of our existence.

Such a demonstration must take nothing for granted that it has not first established. It will start, accordingly, from the most radical negation, and rise progressively, stage by stage, to the most abundant affirmation.

The most radical negation consists in refusing to admit that existence presents any problem at all, because existence can have no meaning, and can therefore raise no problem. This is the nihilist attitude, very widespread these days, and current in several variations. For example, it is contended that existence is absurd or fundamentally precarious, that it has no meaning other than that one chooses to give it, that the profound is only to be discovered in the superficial. These theses merit discussion, if only to show up the internal contradiction they contain.

Once it is admitted that man's existence has a meaning, there will be the temptation to look for it in human activity itself, on this side of the absolute, in an atheistic humanism. Man's existence, it will be suggested, will be fulfilled in his work, in mastering nature with the aid of science and technology, in organizing society on a purely human basis so that man shall recognize nothing superior to mankind and nothing more compelling than human ends. Supreme wisdom will then consist in being conscious of the plenitude of man's achievement. This idea, with its variations, will also have to be discussed. But there is no reason to quarrel with the idea that man finds fulfilment in his own work. The question is whether he can find total fulfilment in it; whether he can realize his true end and destiny in it when he has within his reach a means of access to something that surpasses all his mere humanity could ever achieve. We shall have to show also that in the heart of atheistic humanism there is a yearning for the Absolute that tends to well up and overflow.

We could then go on with our analysis of the human condition at the lowest stage. On the one hand, we have the finiteness of man, who has been thrown into the existent world, condemned to be free in spite of himself, doomed to evil, suffering, frustration and death. On the other hand, we should never be aware of this finiteness if we did not have within us something that would enable us to transcend it. Within us, indeed, the presence of "the one thing necessary", the divine presence, asserts itself. We must give heed to it. We shall have to show that it confronts every man with an inevitable choice—either to ignore this presence of the Absolute Being within us or to open our hearts to him. The negative choice will deprive man of the source of his existence; the positive choice, therefore, is imperative. It will mean submission of oneself to the Absolute who is the source of our existence. This submission implies self-abnegation, and consists, in the long run, in acknowledging that our fulfilment, or rather our encounter with the Absolute—for it is the same thing—can only be given us by the Absolute himself.[5]

Such a dialectic obviously leads up to the idea of a supernatural, as yet vague and undetermined. And now we come to

[5]This is a paraphrase of the classical thesis maintaining that, once God's existence is admitted, we are under the duty to show our faith in him by adopting a religious attitude, and to lay ourselves open to his action, whatever it may be, including an actual experience of divine revelation.

a most important point. This vague, undetermined idea of a supernatural, immanent in every soul conscious of itself, paves the way for the clear, definite idea of the supernatural offered by Christianity. This point cannot be stressed too strongly today when many of our contemporaries find the very idea of a supernatural utterly meaningless. The dialectic that brings out the idea of a supernatural is an invitation, also, to adopt a religious attitude. And this religious attitude, which is already an adumbration of the Christian attitude of faith, is necessary, as we have said, for discernment of the divine revelation.

When it has been shown what our relationship to the Absolute is, and what it ought to be, it remains to demonstrate that Christianity is the historical definition of that relationship. By virtue of this the Christian faith will appear as the condition necessary for man's fulfilment.

To give direction to this demonstration it is useful to bear in mind two things. In the first place, as historicity is an essential quality of the human being, it should be no matter for surprise that man's relationship to the Absolute should be defined in contingent historical events. In the second place, Christianity thinks of itself as a history of signs that have a very special significance. It is founded on a connected sequence of events and a doctrine that declares what they signify; and it is an integral and indissoluble whole. Of these events one is regarded as central and decisive, and around it all the doctrine is disposed. That event is the appearance of Jesus Christ. The Church proclaims Christ and aspires to live by him. It must be shown that the answer to that yearning for the Absolute which every man feels within him is that remarkable organic *ensemble* which is the Church.

This faces us with a twofold task: on the one hand, to show that Christianity views itself as a coherent *ensemble;* on the other, to show that this *ensemble* provides the means of solving the various riddles of man's relation to the Absolute, and enables man to order his life in accordance with that relationship. On one side, we have understanding the faith; on the other, understanding by faith ("faith" being used here in its objective sense of "content of the faith"). The first task is mainly one for dogmatic theology; the second is more proper to apologetics. Both, however, aim at bringing out the rational element in Christianity.

Both of these tasks, it can easily be seen, are complicated in the extreme. True, nobody is required to perform them in full in order to have a rational faith. But it is necessary for the Church as a religious organization in society that these tasks shall be performed, because the Church should be able to render a full account of the faith. Theologians, at least, ought to know and be able to explain, for example, that the dogma of the Trinity is not an algebraic conundrum; it was formulated in order to clarify what the New Testament tells us about Christ, and it enables us, besides, to solve the enigma presented by the idea of a solitary God with no life of his own. Theologians ought to know also, and be able to explain, the human signification of the dogmas of original sin and the redemption, of the eucharistic symbol and the like. In short, they ought to know and be able to explain the *ratio fidei*. In this way they will demonstrate that Christianity, that is to say, Christian life in the bosom of the living Church of Christ, is the historical definition of man's relation to the Absolute.

This demonstration will have established the necessity for man to adhere to Christianity, recognizing it to be God's revelation. But it does not dispense man from freely taking the step demanded by the faith. As we have already said, no reason for believing dispenses from believing. And it is only by experiencing the faith that man can experience the certitude of divine revelation. Apologetical demonstration will, at least, have established that it is not reasonable to refuse experience of the faith.

Furthermore, it is important to note that not only at the end of the demonstration, but also at each stage of its development, free consent is required. The presence of "the one thing necessary" must be freely acknowledged. The inadequacy of atheistic humanism must be freely acknowledged. The nihilist attitude must be freely renounced. Every thesis on the meaning of existence can be contested. But it is important to remember that if the truth cannot be known without being recognized, the truth, none the less, passes judgement on those who fail to recognize it. The need to carry on the dialectic of everyday life does not do away with the need—the spiritual need— immanent in that dialectic.

You by this time will have detected the Blondelian hall-mark on my treatment of this whole subject. As a matter of fact, I do not think anybody has improved on Blondel's definition of what apologetics ought to be in our contemporary world. True, his work has its obscure patches and it is, in quite a number of respects, outdated. But it has dealt with the crucial point so well that we can still learn something from it.[6]

Moreover, no profound knowledge of the history of Christian thought is needed to make one realize that Blondel's work is nourished entirely on traditional fare. St Augustine, St Anselm, St Thomas Aquinas and Pascal have worked on analogous lines, each to meet the particular requirements of his own age.

And what is more, as Blondel himself has pointed out, this method is based on St Paul. The apostle knew that, while the Jews wanted miracles, the pagan Gentiles set store by wisdom,

[6]See our *Blondel et le christianisme*, Paris, 1961.

and it was as divine wisdom that he presented Christianity to them. How does he set about explaining why they ought to believe in Christ? Early in the epistle to the Romans he tells them that the requirements of God's law are already written on Gentile hearts, and that Gentile consciences bear witness to it.[7] He offers adherence to Christ as the authentic means whereby they can recognize God. This is the very procedure I have already pointed out when I said that it must be shown that Christianity gives us the historical definition of man's relationship to the Absolute.

4. *"De Christo legato divino"*

I have now indicated the broad outlines of a logically planned manual on apologetics which would, at the same time, be based on universal principles and related to our contemporary situation. How would such a work compare with the classical treatise "De Christo legato divino" (Christ, God's Envoy), still current in the seminary curriculum?

In the form familiar to us, this treatise is a work that has developed from sixteenth-century origins. Its earliest titles were "On Christian Revelation" or "On the Truth of the Christian Religion" or "On Revealed Religion". Almost from the start, it is to be found sandwiched between two other works, one on religion in general (which became, in the seventeenth century, a treatise on natural religion and the necessity of revelation) and the other on the Catholic religion and the Church of Christ, designed to prove that the Catholic Church was the only one of the various Christian denominations that complied with the intentions of Christ. The object of the treatise on the Christian religion—the *De Christo*—was to demonstrate the truth of that religion from the intrinsic merit of its teaching and the external

---

[7] *Rom.* 2:15.

signs of its divine origin, namely, Christ's miracles and the fulfilment of the prophecies. In short, it was an elaboration of the arguments given in the gospels themselves.

In the course of the nineteenth century, the treatise seems to have been shaken to its foundations; thenceforward its main preoccupation was to make them firm and secure once more. On the one hand, the spread of atheism to a large section of the population did away with the only background against which the gospel arguments had any rational meaning at all. On the other hand, historical criticism, in which rationalism was now prevalent, appeared to have demolished the gospel arguments by calling in question the historical value of the gospels themselves. A twofold task, therefore, seemed imperative. First, the theoretical bases of the treatise had to be consolidated, more attention being paid to the phenomenon of atheism, and more insistence being placed on the possibility of supernatural revelation, of miracles and the like. After that it became the chief function of the treatise to establish, by the use of the historical and critical method, that the gospels were true accounts of what had happened, that they depicted Jesus as, in fact, he had been, that he had really performed the miracles attributed to him, and so on.

All this involved so many complications that the future Cardinal Dechamps felt it necessary to suggest a simpler method: the initial emphasis should be placed on the signs accrediting the divine origin of the Church and from this there should be a gradual transition to Christ as preached by the Church. This method was eventually adopted, but only in part, and the *De Christo* treatise thus modified, retains its place in the curriculum. It continues to go directly to the gospel texts, treating them as ordinary historical documents, and to seek out there the person of Jesus of Nazareth, what he said and what he did, just as it was heard and seen by those that heard

and saw him and—often enough—went their way uncon-
vinced. It was hoped that this objective historical approach
would in time develop into an effective method of justifying
faith in Christ.

But, lo and behold! as the twentieth century went on, first
the Protestant, and then the Catholic exegetes became conscious
that the gospels are not strictly neutral, strictly literal, historical
documents, not exact accounts of what Jesus said and did. A
theological idea and intention animate them throughout. They
do not report what an objective eye-witness would have
remembered about Jesus. They give us, instead, in a highly
specialized literary form, Jesus Christ, Jesus Messiah, Jesus Lord,
as the faith of the original Christian community believed him
to be, commemorated him in their worship, and preached him.
It is only through the faith of these earliest Christians and by
way of the literary *genre* proper to the gospels, that we can
arrive at a historical knowledge of Jesus. The work of discernment is exceedingly delicate, its details are often controversial,
and it must always be carried out with due regard to the very
specialized nature of the gospels.

Seen in the perspective of contemporary scriptural exegesis,
it is obvious that the *De Christo* treatise must be given a new
look, and that its tenor and argumentation must undergo some
modification. It is for the exegetes to say what requirements in
the matter of criticism the apologists must now live up to, and
also what fresh resources are now available to them in this
regard.[8] It is our business as apologists to say how that treatise,
duly renovated—or remade—by the work of the exegetes, falls
in with the concept of faith we have had in mind, and how it
can be inserted in the proposed apologetical work already
outlined. To tell the truth, when the necessary repairs and

[8]See *Bulletin du Comité des Études (de la Compagnie de Saint-Sulpice)*, no. 35
Octobre-Decembre 1961, 311–26.

alterations have been carried out, the venerable treatise will be much more at home there than it is now.

The object of the Christian faith, indeed, is not the figure of Jesus laboriously reconstructed by the historians; it is the figure of Christ preached by the Church, Christ in whom the Church lives, moves, and has her being. The Church, of course, realizes that the Christ of faith is identical with Jesus of Nazareth and that Jesus of Nazareth lived among men and is a historical personage. But the Church is concerned with Jesus considered as the Christ, the Holy One of God, revealed by God. Now we have already seen that there is no revelation that is not revealed to somebody. The revelation manifested in Jesus implies not only the presence of God within him but also the recognition of that presence by those that were witnesses of his life. Accordingly, it is in the faith of the apostles and the original Christian community that God's revelation of Jesus to humanity was made effective. The Church has never failed to realize this down through the ages. On the one hand, indeed, she holds that the history of revelation was brought to a close not by the ascension but by the death of the last of the apostles. On the other hand, it has always considered itself as "apostolic", that is to say, as perpetuating the faith of the apostles. A correct view, therefore, of the relation between revelation and faith puts us in the same perspective as contemporary exegesis of the New Testament: we know Jesus only through the faith of the original Christian community.

But, while the Church presents Christ to us as he appears in the faith of the earliest Christians, she realizes full well that this faith is bound up with the historical reality of Jesus. If historical criticism were to establish that Jesus had conceived himself and his mission differently from what the gospels tell us; if it were to be proved that his message had quite another meaning, that the accounts of his miracles were all literary fabrications, that the fulfilment of the Scriptures in Jesus was only a fancy of the first Christian believers, then Christian preaching would have started out from a fiction and the divine revelation would not be a historical event but a legend. The Church would all along have misconceived her own origin and her preaching would embody a permanent error. It is, then, of the most vital importance to demonstrate that this is not so. Today that is the essential task of *De Christo legato divino*, a task all the more necessary at the present time when a good many non-believers accept the findings of radical criticism, and when even the faithful are disturbed by them.

By itself the treatise *De Christo* would not appear to have the apologetical force so badly needed these days. Neither the miracles of old nor the paradoxical fulfilment of the ancient prophecies would carry much weight with our non-believing contemporaries. Mention of the sanctity of Jesus would be likely to move them only if they were to see Christian sanctity, in imitation of Jesus, openly flourishing in our own time. Likewise, the gospel message that is likely to arouse their interest is the Church's contemporary teaching of the doctrine of the New Testament, rather than the message of Jesus reconstructed by historians. And the *De Christo* alone, in present circumstances, can have little effect in furthering recognition of Christianity as the historical definition of man's relation to the Absolute.

None the less, the venerable classical treatise, suitably modified as we have said, has an essential role in such a demonstration. For it is of very great consequence indeed to establish that Christianity is not under a delusion as to what it is, when it proclaims and prizes beyond measure its attachment to the historical figure of Jesus.

This last-mentioned and most important point cannot be established by the historical and critical method. In theory, of course, that method, being scientific, ought to afford results that would be valid in the eyes of every historian, Catholic, Protestant, or uncommitted. But it is all too true that, on a good many important points, even on some essential points, exegetes have been led, by their belief or unbelief, to different conclusions. Are we to despair, then, of ever reaching conclusions, by the scientific historical method, that will carry general conviction? Must we admit that the work to which we devote our lives is only capable of convincing the convinced?

Contemporary theories of historical knowledge, for example, those of Raymond Aron, H. I. Marrou and others, show very clearly that such knowledge necessarily comprises a subjective element. The French Revolution is not depicted in the same manner by a royalist and by a republican. We need not be surprised, then, if the history of Jesus is not reconstructed in the same manner by a Catholic, by a liberal Protestant and by a non-believer.

But let us not conclude from this that historical knowledge can never be objective, that is to say, can never arrive at universally valid results. Raymond Aron once said that objectivity in history is defined by the dialogue of historians. The objective then emerges as what is accepted by the generality of historians who take one another seriously. There are, indeed, many things on which historians have reached agreement after dialogue.

Agreement of this kind is what we ought to envisage in the historical exegesis of the New Testament. If Catholic exegetes were to be alone in maintaining, even in the name of historical method, standpoints universally and definitively rejected by other exegetes, they would be placed in a delicate position. It might very well seem to those around them that they were not speaking in the name of historical science, but in the name of

their faith. Their failure to say something that carried weight
with incredulous minds would mean that their work would
have no apologetical impact.

It is of great consequence that those who teach the *De Christo
legato divino* should take care not to pin their faith on the
apologetical efficacy of statements universally contested outside the Catholic world. Even if they set store by them, let
them not base apologetical argument on violently controversial material. Let them rely rather on what is accepted by
the generality of serious exegetes. Let us never confuse what
we can, or ought to, admit among ourselves, with what we
can establish by scientific historical method. In this way only
can we say something that means something to those who do
not believe. If, by confining ourselves to this rigorous procedure, we should succeed in getting our message across to
others, they, too, may eventually come to accept by faith
what we ourselves accept in faith.

We have seen how conviction of our faith is born of a vague
experience of revelation that is itself implicit in the faith.
We have seen, too, how this can be made explicit in an
apologetical work capable of helping souls along the road to
faith.

It will have been observed that the work we have outlined
utilizes both the reflections of the philosopher and the labours
of the historian. It brings out, on the one hand, the structure of
the reasoning process implied in the act of faith, and, on the
other hand, the historical event from which Christianity
springs. These are two tasks that must be undertaken if we are
to demonstrate that Christianity is the historical definition of
our relation to the Absolute.

In so far as it concerns the faithful, it would be better if, as
I have suggested, the manual of apologetics we have been
planning here were to be described as a manual of fundamental

theology. The reason should be now clear. It would supply the fundamentals to which dogmatic and moral theology must always return. For it would enshrine the true sense of dogma and the logical basis, the rationale, of Christian life.

II

THE LIBERTY OF THE CHRISTIAN

When a Christian tries to think and write in accordance with truth, and to preserve in everything he does a rational balance between justice and efficiency, he is apt to feel—if he is really intent on living his faith—that the doctrinal, moral and disciplinary demands of his religion put obstacles in his way, slow him up, and set up a nagging conflict of thoughts and emotions within him. He experiences the feeling that he is being robbed of his liberty. Who or what instigates such a sentiment? Is it the Spirit of God who created man to his own image, yet endowed him with reason and the free and un-fettered use of it? Is it the spirit symbolized by the serpent of the earthly paradise, inviting him to make himself like to God? In other words, is there such a thing as Christian liberty and, if there is, what is it?

1. *The Teaching of St Paul*

If we open the New Testament, especially at the writings of St Paul and St John, we find that the question of liberty keeps on cropping up. In admitting man's responsibility, the New Testament takes this as implying what philosophers call a power of choice, or better still, an original or primal liberty by which man is the cause of, and bears the responsibility for, his actions. But the New Testament does not say this in so many words. Indeed, what it calls liberty is "perfect" liberty, that is, the condition of the Christian who is set free from the servitude of sin and lives in communion with God through Christ and the holy Spirit. The "liberty of the children of God" of which St Paul speaks (*Rom.* 8:21) is the life "to God in Christ Jesus" (*Rom.* 6:10–11).

We should never forget this, when we think of the liberty of the Christian. However, the question we are concerned with here is not quite the same. We are now dealing with liberty in relation to authority, and primarily to religious authority, to the law or the commandment of God defined by the Church. The New Testament doctrine by which we should be guided in this matter is that formulated by St Paul when he declared that the Christian is set free from the law, is free with regard to the law.

This doctrine is interpreted differently by Catholics, Lutherans and Calvinists; within each denomination, indeed, various interpretations are current. If we want to arrive at an exact understanding of St Paul's thought, perhaps we should first forget these differences, go directly to the text, and see what we can make of it ourselves.

"We hold," says St Paul in the epistle to the Romans, "that a man is justified by faith apart from works of law" (*Rom.* 3:28). Since Luther, this has often been regarded as a simple, *formal* antithesis between faith and works, while the sacred author envisages a *historical* antithesis as well between two consecutive divine dispensations—the Mosaic law and the Christian faith. For Paul, in fact, and for all the New Testament

writers, the appearance of Christ and the gift of the holy
Spirit to Christian believers give rise to a new phenomenon in
the spiritual history of mankind, a phenomenon that divides
it into two eras. "But *now*," he says, "the righteousness of God
has been manifested apart from law, although the law and the
prophets bear witness to it, the righteousness of God through
faith in Jesus Christ for all who believe" (*Rom.* 3:21-22). This
"was to prove *at the present time* that he (God) himself is
righteous" (*Rom.* 3:26). With Christ the law *came to an end*,
for he himself is the principle of righteousness for "everyone
who has faith" (*Rom.* 10:4). In another place he says, "When
we were children, we were slaves to the elemental spirits of the
universe. But *when the time had fully come*, God sent forth his
Son, born of woman, born under the law, to redeem those
who were under the law, so that we might receive adoption
as sons" (*Gal.* 4:3-4). A Protestant exegete, following in the
wake of other interpreters, put it excellently: "Paul is conscious
of living in an absolutely new era, inaugurated by a new
'judgement' of God, which necessitated a new response from
man."[1] The antithesis Paul sets up between justification by
faith and justification by the law signifies, therefore, the
substitution of a new, for an old, dispensation. When he
asserts that man is justified by faith and not by the works of
the law, he means that salvation not only comes from God,
but is transmitted henceforth through Christianity, and not,
as hitherto, through Judaism.

It was the demands of the judaizing Christians that gave him
the chance to clarify his views on the law. Converts from
Judaism demanded that Jewish religious observance down to
the smallest detail should be imposed on Christian converts

---

[1]Pierre Bonnard, *L'Épître de saint Paul aux Galates*, Neuchatel-Paris, 1953,
122.

from paganism; this would make the latter subject to the
Jewish prescriptions as to circumcision, the sabbath, festivals,
purification and so on. In the epistle to the Galatians, Paul
addresses himself to these doctrinaires and to those who had
been led astray by them. "A man," he says, "is not justified
by works of the law but through faith in Jesus Christ . . . by
works of the law shall no one be justified" (*Gal.* 2:16). "If
justification were through the law, then Christ died to no
purpose" (*Gal.* 2:21). "Now before faith came, we (born
Jews) were confined under the law, kept under restraint until
faith should be revealed. So that the law was our custodian until
Christ came, that we might be justified by faith. But now that
faith has come, we are no longer under a custodian; for in
Christ Jesus you are all sons of God, through faith. . . . There
is neither Jew nor Greek . . . for you are all one in Christ
Jesus" (*Gal.* 3:23–28). "For freedom Christ has set us free;
stand fast therefore, and do not submit again to a yoke of
slavery . . . if you receive circumcision, Christ will be of no
advantage to you . . . You are severed from Christ, you who
would be justified by the law; you have fallen away from
grace" (*Gal.* 5:1–4).

Paul asserts, therefore, that it is derogatory to Christ to hold
that observance of the law is necessary for justification or
salvation. Are we then to conclude that he would free Christians
from every obligation towards it? Listen to what he says later
on in the same epistle: "For you were called to freedom,
brethren; only do not use your freedom as an opportunity for
the flesh, but through love be servants of one another. For the
whole law is fulfilled in one word: 'You shall love your
neighbour as yourself'" (*Gal.* 5:13–14). And so the law in so
far as it can be summed up as charity, continues to be obligatory
for the Christian. It is the "law of Christ" (*Gal.* 6:2). And its
observance is the condition for attaining salvation at the last

judgement, for "whatever a man sows, that he will also reap" (*Gal.* 6:7). Paul obviously does not mean to exempt the Christian from every obligation towards the law; in his eyes, the law somehow continues to stand for one of God's abiding claims on man.

But then, what does he mean when he declares, by and large, that the Christian is set free from the law? He means that the Christian is not subject to the law in all the exacting details of Jewish observance. The Christian convert from paganism does not need to become a Jew and submit to circumcision and the other legal observances that distinguish Jew from pagan. Even the Christian convert from Judaism is no longer held to these observances, because, on the coming of Christ, observance of the *distinctive elements* of Jewish religious practice became obsolete. That is one of the essential points of St Paul's teaching. It is difficult to realize today how revolutionary it seemed, not alone to the Jews, but to the ex-Jewish Christians. The disciples of the apostle James refused to accept it. Peter himself had accepted it in principle but dared not put it into practice when he happened to find himself among Judaizers. When the latter were not about, he did not hesitate to eat with pagans; when the doctrinaires were present, he returned to Jewish practices. Paul publicly rebuked him for this lack of firmness, which could have the effect of troubling consciences: "If you, though a Jew, live like a Gentile and not like a Jew, how can you compel the Gentiles to live like Jews?" (*Gal.* 2:14).

Paul's conviction is based on the idea that Christ's redemption avails for all mankind, pagans as well as Jews, and that the principle of salvation is the same for all, faith in Christ. If, to be saved, it were necessary to observe the Jewish law, only the Jews would be saved. The epistle to the Ephesians has some striking passages that set out Paul's universalism in the clearest

terms. "The mystery was made known to me by revelation . . .
how the Gentiles are fellow heirs, members of the same body,
and partakers of the promise in Christ Jesus" (*Eph.* 3:3–6).
"Remember that at one time, you Gentiles in the flesh, called
the uncircumcision by what is called the circumcision, which
is made in the flesh by hands—remember that you were at that
time separated from Christ, alienated from the commonwealth
of Israel, and strangers to the covenants of promise, having no
hope and without God in the world. But now in Christ Jesus
you who once were far off have been brought near in the
blood of Christ. For he is our peace, who has made us both
one, and *has broken down the dividing wall of hostility, by abolishing
in his flesh the law of commandments and ordinances,* that he might
create in himself one new man in place of the two . . . and
might reconcile us both to God in one body through the cross,
thereby bringing the hostility to an end" (*Eph.* 2:11–15).
Accordingly, under the dispensation inaugurated by Christ's
death, salvation is no longer deemed to be reserved for the
Jews; it is extended to all who believe in Christ, Jews and
pagans united in one and the same body. The law of Moses,
to be sure, is abolished—but only in a very special sense. It is
abolished only *to the extent that its precepts and ordinances raise
a barrier between Jews and pagans.* There is no reason why it
should not continue in force where its content coincides with
the natural law written on pagan hearts. We find this partial
coincidence of Jewish and natural law expressly mentioned by
Paul in the epistle to the Romans (*Rom.* 2:14–15). How moving
it is to see this Jew—who had been so passionately attached
to everything that distinguished him from the pagans
—renounce his distinctive Jewish privileges from the
moment Christ opened his eyes! The only vestiges of
the Jewish law he wanted to retain were those spontaneously practised by the good pagan. All the rest he

declared to be outmoded; the Christian is freed from it.[2]

Today we might say that all this is obvious and that, in any event, Christian liberty would be a very scanty privilege indeed if it consisted only in being exempt from specific observances of Judaism. True enough, but Paul went farther than that. The "freedom" he preaches in the epistle to the Galatians implies more than exemption from certain practices; it implies also freedom from Jewish legalism. This has a more general bearing on our own contemporary attitude and behaviour.

The sect of the Pharisees, to which Paul belonged before his conversion, tended to regard the law as a collection of unrelated precepts imposed from outside (as distinct from immanent "natural law"). This code (an inexact but convenient word!) had to be observed down to the last and most minute detail of its exacting requirements. The same importance was attached to each individual precept in it. There was, for example, a tendency to place a detail of the purification ritual on the same footing as the ordinance regulating respect for human life. Omission to observe some detail of prescribed practice out of ignorance or forgetfulness was held to be not less reprehensible before God than deliberate neglect. The idea of obedience was formal in the extreme; recourse was had to such formalism to get round inconvenient precepts.

We know, from the gospels, that Jesus often strongly criticized the attitude of the Pharisees and their method of interpreting the law. He took up the themes of the prophets and attacked this hypocritical formalism and the legalist conception on which it rested. He reduced the law to one only among its many precepts: love of God and one's neighbour.

Paul makes much of this idea, reiterating it with vigorous

[2]This is gone into at greater length in our work *Karl Barth*, II, 81–98.

emphasis. He sees that the multifarious precepts of the law spring from, and come back to, the single commandment of love. "For the whole law is fulfilled in one word, 'You shall love your neighbour as yourself'" (*Gal.* 5:14). Now love is no external norm; it is an internal dynamism, a principle both of judgement and of action. Then again, this dynamism is the "fruit of the Spirit" (*Gal.* 5:22), of the divine Spirit's action on the Christian's heart. For the believer, it is no longer a question of observing a code, but of letting himself be guided by the Spirit within him. The legalist attitude gives place to a spiritual process. In this sense, too, the Christian is set free from the law: "But if you are led by the Spirit you are not under the law" (*Gal.* 5:18).

St Paul goes on to explain that this freedom *vis-à-vis* the law must not be made a pretext for indulging desires of the flesh, that is to say, satisfying one's own cravings at the expense of others. Love, and not selfishness, must be our inspiration. And there is nothing so demanding as the love that puts us at the service of our neighbour. But this urge of love to serve others is immanent in every Christian; he has only to let it have its way. When the seat of the law is in one's own soul, submission ceases to be slavery; subjection to an outside power is succeeded by self-government.

"Where the Spirit of the Lord is, there is freedom" (2 *Cor.* 3:17). St Thomas Aquinas makes the following comment on this text:

> He that acts spontaneously, acts freely; but he who acts at the behest of another, does not act freely. When, therefore, the latter avoids evil not because it is evil, but because of a commandment of the Lord, he is not free. On the contrary, he is free who avoids evil because it is evil. Now, that is the work of the holy Spirit, who

perfects our spirit and imparts a new dynamism to it, so
that it refrains from evil out of love, just as if the divine
law itself had commanded it to do so; and in that way it
is free, not that it ceases to be amenable to the divine law,
but because its internal dynamism inclines it to do what
the divine law prescribes.[3]

The Christian, accordingly, is free *vis-à-vis* the law in the
sense that he is freed from legalism. He knows that every
commandment springs ultimately from love, and his faith
inspires him with that love. He has the law within his own
breast; he now does of his own accord, what he is commanded
to do. He judges and acts in collaboration with God.

2. *The Logic of Christian Liberty*

Admittedly some (perhaps many!) people are sometimes
tempted to ask themselves whether the Church has really
remained faithful to St Paul's teaching, whether she has not
curbed—or even entirely suppressed—the liberty of the
Christian. In the catechism classes, in sermons, in theological
courses, rules and regulations proliferate, and so do instructions
on the manner of their application in particular circumstances.
From time to time, also, orders and condemnations issue from
the ecclesiastical authority. The Christian's life seems to be
meticulously prescribed for him by other people. He is told
what he should read, and what he should not read; how he
should behave in his intimate home life, and even (in some
places) what trade union or similar body he should choose
and what political party is taboo. Surely all this is very far
removed from that one and only commandment of love! Have

[3]*In 2 Cor.*, cap. 3, lect. 3.

we not reverted to a legalism and a code suspiciously like that of the Jewish law? What has become of Christian liberty?

It must be freely admitted that Christian morality and Christian education are susceptible of being presented and practised in a manner that endangers Christian liberty. A series of rules, for example, is imposed and remains completely external to those for whom they are intended, because they are not adequately explained and, therefore, are not adequately assimilated. They may be observed solely for fear of the consequences. Moreover, the impression may be given that everything is forbidden—or forbidden at least until specific permission is granted! Children brought up in such circumstances have little chance of ever acquiring adult minds. All their lives they will be plagued by anxiety, if, indeed, they do not throw over all traces of Christian morality—which is another instance of inability to grow up. If we want to preserve the liberty of the Christian, we must guard against all attempts to impose a law and give it divine status, without indicating how the moral conscience can recognize that it is a divine law. We must also rid ourselves of the idea that we should presume to prescribe so mechanical a method of applying the law that consciences would be dispensed from taking on themselves the responsibility for their own judgements.

However, a little theological reflection points the way of escape from such stuffy abuses into the fresh air of liberty.

The Church keeps before our mind the "commandments of God" and clarifies them by her own commandments, in accordance with the divine authority and guarantee. If the commandments were merely arbitrary, submission would be slavery. It is of prime importance, therefore, to grasp the fact that they are not arbitrary, that they mean something, that they express an intelligible necessity. One acts freely when one knows that what one does has a rational meaning.

But, first of all, why on earth should anybody allow himself
to be horrified by the very idea of commandment? In morals,
a commandment is a short cut. There is good ground even for
regarding it as an indispensable element in the exercise of
liberty. The imperative mood is a useful abridgement of a
long-winded process. When we do not want to begin all over
again to explain the basic objects of life and human realities
that must be attended to, we use the imperative mood to save
time and trouble.[4] But the commandment so given points
out the meaning of certain kinds of human behaviour; it
defines the logic of liberty.

In fact, liberty is not realized in any way whatever. It can
achieve its end only by introducing into its projects a coherence,
a logic, that assures their realization. It is in that, precisely, that
morality consists. It establishes between our initiative and our
world a relationship that has a coherent, rational meaning.
Now our world is, in the first place, our neighbour. Human
existence is merged entirely in the interplay of subjective
human minds and personalities. That is why it is of prime
importance for Christian morals to define the coherence, the
rationality of human relationships; directly or indirectly, this
promotes the recognition of man by man.

The Greeks had a name for this recognition of man by
man—*philia* (φιλία). Christianity calls it charity. Charity is the
active recognition of man by man, inspired, however, by a
deeper motive than the pagans knew. It proceeds from faith
in Christ; it knows that man is created in the image of God
and is destined to participate in the life of God. It reflects the
recognition of man by God, who has been revealed to us in
Jesus Christ. Charity, then, is recognition of divine grace and

[4]E. Ortigues, "Sur la théorie psychologique et la réflexion morale", in
Recherches et Débats, no. 3, 169.

by that very fact is also the simultaneous mutual recognition
of God and man. St Paul, following Christ's own teaching,
has shown us how the whole of the law is summed up in one
commandment, the commandment of charity. And our
analysis of what is implied by the idea of commandment in the
moral sphere has come to the same conclusion, which, in a
word, is—charity.

Now the imperative of Christian morality refers to a *divine*
commandment, or to a commandment that is guaranteed by
divine authority. But this adjective "divine" surely re-intro-
duces an outside authority that could be arbitrary or at least
incapable of being reconciled with the exercise of liberty? Here
we must again reflect a little, this time on a thesis well known
to, but not always well used by, Catholic theologians and
philosophers: I mean the doctrine of analogy.

When we affirm that God exists; that God *is* in such-and-such
a way; that God does such-and-such a thing; the terms we use
have not the same meaning as when we use them in reference
to creatures, because God is absolutely transcendent. But
neither are the meanings of the terms in each case *totally*
different; if they were, we should be guilty of equivocation.
Accordingly, when we apply to God terms we can legitimately
apply to man, we use these terms by way of analogy. By
analogy here we do not mean a vague resemblance. Analogy,
in the technical sense, is a process of negation and eminence
based on the dependent relationship of the creature to its
Source.[5]

When, for example, we say that God is good, we know that
he is not good in the manner in which men are good. For the
moment, then, we have to leave aside our ordinary human use

[5]We have explained the Thomist doctrine of analogy in *Karl Barth*, III,
198–204.

of language and say that, from the viewpoint mentioned in our last sentence, God is not good. This negation, however, simply indicates that God is good in an eminent sense, he is eminently good, his goodness is such that we can find no words for it. We know that God is the source of everything; it is because of our dependence on him, indeed, that we can mention him at all.

But let us come to the main point that concerns us in all this. When we are told that God commands this or that, we must not forget that this is the language of analogy, that is to say, it conceals a negation and refers to a relationship. Strictly speaking, God does not command; what we call a commandment is based upon the fact of God's existence and of our relationship to him; it would be better described as a demand for rational human conduct. This demand is conceived and formulated by men; and man, too, is fully aware that it originates with God. Consequently, nothing ought to be imposed, in the name of God, that cannot be justified from the viewpoint of man; but everything that is demanded by the logic of human relations is, precisely on that account, a commandment of God.

And so we see that the notion of divine authority, rightly understood, is not incompatible with the notion of human liberty, because it is an integral element of the logic that governs the proper exercise of human liberty.

If God's commandment defines the logic of liberty in simple terms, why, it will be asked, does Catholic moral doctrine have so many and such detailed general rules? Would it not be more in line with human reality—and St Paul's teaching—if it were to be left to each individual to decide on the proper thing to do *in each particular case, under the guidance of the holy Spirit*, due regard being had to the various ways in which people usually behave, and to the requirements of charity? In other words, would it not be advisable to substitute situational for casuistical, ethical principles? Surely God's commandment is always individual and concrete, envisaging the behaviour of *this* particular man, in *these* circumstances, in *this* case involving *him?*

Situational ethics, indeed, are no novelty in traditional moral doctrine. It has always been taken for granted that the formal statement of moral laws does not free the conscience from responsibility for its own decision in a concrete situation. There are, of course, simple cases where a universal precept is directly and automatically applicable. If a competitor causes me serious injury, I know very well that I have no right to take his life on that account. But that does not help me to decide what I am to do to protect myself against him, without, in my turn, doing him an injury. Most cases, indeed, are far from simple; no general rule could cover them. Several rules have to be applied simultaneously, and it is a matter for the fine instinct of an individual's conscience to discern their relevance to the situation. This fine instinct of conscience (or "tact" of conscience) is what the medieval theologians used to call the virtue of prudence. It was not the art of dodging risk and trouble; it meant alert judgement, alive to the nature of things, and did not shrink, on occasion, from applying bold measures. It was also generally admitted that, even when one's conscience was mistaken, its decision was binding, provided one acted in good faith. If someone, said St Thomas, thinks he should curse Christ, it will be his duty to curse Christ. It is the judgement of each conscience in each particular situation that comes nearest to the norm of morality.

But that does not justify us in throwing general precepts overboard—as certain types of situational ethics seem intent on doing. Where they go wrong is in pretending that there is a radical opposition between a universal rule and a concrete exigency, that these are mutually exclusive. If the concrete exigency, that is, the pressing need of the moment, is not wholly arbitrary, it is intelligible, it has a meaning. Now every meaning is certainly concrete inasmuch as it is immanent in a concrete situation. But every meaning has a formal aspect also, and can, therefore, be expressed in universal terms. What God requires of us is always some particular act; his command-ment is a concrete definition. And so, because it has a meaning (like the action prescribed by it) it has both a universal and a particular aspect. Admittedly it is when one is personally involved in a concrete situation that one discerns the principles which determine it and, when acted upon, give one's human act its moral value. But the principles so discerned are universal principles, susceptible of being expressed in general rules. Rightly understood, the definition of a general law and its method of application in particular cases is a matter of bringing out the ultimate reason why an individual action falls logically into place in an authentic relationship of human personalities. General rules exist because liberty and charity are not arbitrary things, because there is a logic of liberty and of human relation-ships. How could these rules be replaced, as some suggest, by the inspiration of the holy Spirit when it is they that help us to discern which of our inspirations come from the holy Spirit, and which emanate from our own egoism?

But we must repeat that the official statement of these rules and the directives of moralists as to their application, do not dispense us from discerning by ourselves, perhaps with the help of an adviser, what they mean, and what they prescribe for us in a particular situation. We are never relieved from the effort and responsibility involved in making our own decision.

In this sense, we are always free. But our freedom has always to be fought for, and that is something we cannot afford to forget. We are perpetually tempted to confuse this freedom

with the caprice of instinct. We have to keep constantly
clarifying and refining our consciences so as to ensure the
rationality of our relations with others and the rationality of
the relations between the different elements of our own
personality. The logic of our liberty is realized only through
repeated victories over the blind violence of our instincts.

Up to now I have been dealing with liberty in relation to
the moral law. I should like also to say a few words about the
Christian's liberty with regard to decisions or specific directives
issued from time to time by the ecclesiastical authority,
particularly on political matters. The problem here is somewhat different. But here, too, we ought to be guided by the
logic of the situation.

Theologians no longer contend that the Church has an
intrinsic power, directly exercisable, in temporal affairs. Popes
do not now claim the right to appoint and depose rulers or to
abrogate civil laws. It is agreed that the State is sovereign in its
own domain and that the Church has no temporal jurisdiction
there. Consequently, heads of state, ministers and members of
parliament have complete freedom of action in their own
spheres, even if they are Catholics. Their norm is the common
good. The same applies to citizens in their political activities,
such as exercising their voting rights, writing on political
topics or working on behalf of a political party.

Nevertheless, the Church claims the power of binding
consciences, even in temporal matters, when these have also
an inherently spiritual aspect. This claim is exercised primarily,
in a very general way, by issuing periodical reminders to the
faithful with respect to the basic principles of justice and
charity which ought to regulate political and social life. The
Church also intervenes expressly to condemn, and defend
herself against, a law or regime that seeks to impair the Church's
spiritual rights, or to restrict the freedom of Christians to lead

a Christian life, or, less specifically, to interfere with the individual citizen's liberty. It is in this context that the Church has officially condemned atheistic communism, fascism and national socialism. When she stresses the primary principles of justice and respect for spiritual values, and condemns a regime or an ideology which would directly violate them, it is evident that the Catholic is bound to listen and obey. But his obedience does not exempt him from the free and responsible exercise of his initiative, all the more because the enunciation of general principles or the condemnation of an ideology is not likely to prove an adequate determinant as regards the best action that can be taken in any concrete situation. As to the technical method or means of attaining to a greater degree of social justice in this or that undertaking or country, that is for the responsible parties to work out for themselves, while taking account of the possibilities of time and place. How a Christian living under a communist regime is to behave in such-and-such a situation can very often be decided only by himself. He will have regard to the Church's directives but also to the possibilities that still remain open to him. His choice, God knows, will not always be easy.

It sometimes happens that the Church's condemnation is aimed not at an atheistic or anti-Christian ideology, but at the political trends of a group of Catholics. At the beginning of this century, the Church condemned the French democratic movement called *Le Sillon*. More recently she issued a warning against progressivism, whose aim was to effect a synthesis of Christianity and Marxism. These ecclesiastical interventions are all the more painful because they involve Catholics who are unquestionably animated by a spirit of generosity. Even when the Church's condemnations are not too happily worded, an endeavour should be made to appreciate what justifies, or at least explains, them. The objects of Christian generosity, too, are not always clearly envisaged, and may need to be clarified. Catholics should not allow themselves to be discouraged by the Church's disapproval; it should be regarded rather in the light of an invitation to reconsider and adjust opinions and attitudes. The leaders and members of *Le Sillon* understood, and modified certain parts of their programme, and the Church later gave her specific approval to the type of Christian democracy that derived from that movement. Liberty and authority, having each revised its position, were brought back into concord.

Another set of circumstances calls for mention. It may happen that the ecclesiastical authority does not rest content with recalling universally valid principles or condemning movements which directly attack Christianity or certain spiritual values. She may expressly recommend a certain political orientation, a party, a trade association or the like. The Vatican itself does something of this kind occasionally, but more usually such recommendations come direct from the bishops (or even from the parish priests). This type of pronouncement causes extreme embarrassment to the faithful, who may, in all good faith, find that it is unfortunate from the political and social points of view. How are they to exercise their liberty in so delicate a situation? If they are well-informed on political and social affairs, they will prefer the course dictated by their own conscience. If, at the same time, they take their religion seriously, they will be anxious to pay due respect to the ecclesiastical authority and to give no ground for scandal to their weaker brethren. The first step they should take in such circumstances might be to enlighten the authority on the matter in dispute. The second should be to proceed calmly and discreetly, avoiding impulsive action. If they are confronted by a choice between two evils, let them take the lesser. What further general rules can we lay down? Each case has to stand on its own legs. The authority may have exceeded its jurisdiction and issued an unfortunate directive. But it also happens that the individuals concerned in such cases may lose sight of the general good of the Church or of human society. The exercise of liberty certainly demands clear-headedness, courage, and a rather modest opinion of one's own merits.

Having considered Christian liberty in the realm of action, we might now be expected to consider how it operates in the intellectual sphere. To what extent does Catholic dogma give Catholics genuine freedom to think, theorize and investigate for themselves? This question obviously does not arise at all in departments of thought which have no relevance to the faith, such as mathematics and physics, for example, psychology, history, technical studies and so on. But it could arise in disciplines that border on the domains of faith and dogma, such as philosophy, anthropology and similar fields. And, having gone into this question, we could go still more deeply into the whole matter and inquire how dogma itself can be merged integrally in our own thought.

We shall limit ourselves here to a reference to the principle of responses. Dogma is the ecclesiastical expression of the mystery of our relationship to God as he has been revealed in Jesus Christ. Dogma, therefore, has a meaning, a meaning that concerns us, and, what is more, a meaning that we can see concerns us. That is why dogma can, in its own way, become incorporated with our thought and, indeed, stimulate and fertilize it. We can be certain that the task of the thinking Christian is not always an easy one; it comes up against many difficulties, from within and from without. But brave effort always succeeds somehow in struggling through the dark tunnel of doubt and difficulty into the light of truth.

We can now sum up. There is such a thing as Christian liberty and we have seen how it is determined. We should like to repeat that it has always to be fought for; it is to be had only at the cost of constant victories over the blind urges of caprice and instinct. We must particularly bear in mind one thing that we learned at the very outset of our inquiry: the true fulfilment of liberty consists of communion with God. "For all things are yours," says St Paul, "whether the world or life or death or the present or the future, all are yours; and you are Christ's; and Christ is God's" (1 *Cor.* 3:21–23).

PART TWO

Dialogues with Protestant Thought

III

THE FAITH ACCORDING TO KIERKEGAARD

The rise of existential philosophies and the rapid development of dialectical theology have alike helped to reinstate that
strange thinker, Sören Kierkegaard (1813–1855) in public
esteem. Numerous translations have made his work more
widely accessible, and sound commentaries continue to make
it more intelligible.[1] During the past few years, no doubt,
existentialism has suffered a set-back, and we now hear rather
less of him. But his ideas are not dead by any means. It would
be hard to avoid coming up against them—and having it out
with them—in any serious study of the uniqueness of the
gospel message, the ways of approach to the faith, and the
difficulty of "becoming a Christian".

Philosophers interested in Kierkegaard's ideas have occasionally been tempted to concentrate on such elements of his

---

[1]We have to thank Jean Wahl for the first comprehensive account in the
French language of Kierkegaard's work as a whole. His *Études kierkegaardiennes*
(Aubier, 1938, re-issued by Vrin in 1949) is still one of the best works on the
subject. Also recommended, Mgr R. Jolivet, *Aux sources de l'existentialisme
chrétien: Kierkegaard*, new edn., Paris 1958.

thought as can be secularized, for example, existence, subjectivity, anguish, the absurd, opposition to "system". But it
would be quite wrong to forget that his thought always moves
in and around the interior life of man, and the Christian faith,
faith in the Man-God. This faith he treated as the apex of
existence. His thought would be completely unintelligible if
its genesis were not kept in mind.

Reading contributed very little to the shaping of his
philosophy; nearly all of his ideas were the products of his own
personal experience. He had, indeed, been a theological student.
But far more important in his formation were the austere kind
of Christianity, and the terrible confidences, he had received
from his father; these had developed in him an anxious awareness of sin. His relations with his fiancée—which seem so disconcerting to us—sharpened his sense of inwardness, of secret
things, of indirect communication. Finally, a personal reaction
against the allurements of romanticism and Hegelianism
impelled him to devote himself to the study of Christianity
and the implications of the Christian life.

Nearly all his works tell us something about his conception
of faith. His "Concluding Unscientific Postscript" will concern
us most. But to interpret it rightly and to round it off, we
would refer the reader to "Philosophical Fragments", "Training in Christianity", "Fear and Trembling", and, above all,
to the "Journal".[2]

---

[2]Translator's note: *Post-scriptum aux Miettes philosophiques, Miettes philosophiques, École du Christianisme, Crainte et tremblement*, and the *Journal* have
been translated into English under the following titles respectively: *Concluding Unscientific Postscript* (tr. D. F. Swenson and W. Lowrie), London
1941; *Philosophical Fragments* (tr. D. F. Swenson), New York 1936; *Training
in Christianity* (tr. W. Lowrie), London 1941; *Fear and Trembling* (tr. R.
Payne), London 1939; *The Journals of Sören Kierkegaard*, a selection edited and
translated by A. Dru, London 1938. References in the notes below are to these
translations, save where otherwise stated.

The kernel of Kierkegaard's thought is that faith is neither a system of speculative philosophy nor a jumping-off ground for such a system; it is a relationship between persons, the connection of one existence with another. It is a decision of the subject and a transcendence, an aspiration, towards the Absolute Other. It is the contact of human subjectivity with the paradox of the Man-God. Subjectivity, paradox—these are its two most characteristic traits.

We know that Kierkegaard's existential thought was a reaction against the Hegelian system. Commentators are now at pains to point out that he was unjust to Hegel by exaggerating the abstract character of Hegel's philosophy, and by failing to recognize the practical value of the principle of mediation. But we should do well to note also that the Hegelianism envisaged by Kierkegaard was not that of the "Phenomenology"; it was the system as interpreted by certain disciples of Hegel, who based it on their recollection of what he had said when they sat under him. More particularly, it was the rationalism that Hegel's philosophy had insinuated into the minds of the Danish theologians of Kierkegaard's time, and that hotch-potch of speculation and bourgeois conformity to which some of them would reduce the message of Christ. Hegelianism, to Kierkegaard's mind, made Christianity so ridiculously easy that anybody could call himself a Christian. For his own part, he would set about showing how difficult it was to become a Christian.

Hegel, he said, spoiled everything by reducing faith to a mere moment of pure thought, and Christianity to a petty system of speculative philosophy, whereas it was really an existential message demanding to be realized in existence—to be lived. With a mixture of the serious and the playful, reminiscent of Plato, the Danish philosopher thus describes the gist of his thought. "I thought to myself: 'You are now tired of life's diversions; you are tired of the maidens, whom you love only in passing; you must have something fully to occupy your time. Here it is: to discover where the misunderstanding lies between speculative philosophy and Christianity.' This therefore became my resolve. . . . My many failures I need not recite here, but finally it became clear to me that the misdirection of speculative philosophy and its consequent assumed justification for reducing faith to the status of a relative moment, could not be anything accidental, but must be rooted deeply in the entire tendency of the age . . . in the fact that on account of our vastly increased knowledge, men had forgotten what it means to *exist* and what *inwardness* signifies."[3] Farther on, the author adds: "If men had forgotten what it means to exist religiously, they had also doubtless forgotten what it means to exist as human beings; this must therefore be set forth."[4] From this we see how Kierkegaard's consciousness of the unique quality of religious faith gives him a starting-point for his existential thought. (In this respect, the development of his thought resembles that of Gabriel Marcel.) We will not go into Kierkegaard's concept of an existential relation between aesthetics and ethics. We will confine ourselves to the religious aspect.

Faith is not speculative philosophizing by the thinking subject. It is distinguished by the infinite interest the individual existent subject takes in his eternal happiness, an interest that transforms his whole existence. The believer is passionately solicitous for his eternal salvation and orients all his life towards the attainment of that absolute good. Faith, therefore, is not disinterested knowledge of an object towards which we are quite indifferent; it means the fervour of passion, decision, engagement. In other words, it is subjectivity, existence.

[3]*Concluding Unscientific Postscript*, 216.
[4]*Ibid.*, 223.

There are two ways of approach to truth, the objective and the subjective. We take the objective way when we want to reach truth in the exact sciences such as mathematics, physics and so on. In that domain, objective truth is reached instantly and with certainty, and there is no question of personal engagement on the part of the subject. But, be it noted, the truth in such cases is a matter of indifference to us; we have no feeling for or against it. On the other hand, where our existence is concerned, in the moral and religious domain, we cannot gain access to truth by the objective method; we have to proceed by the subjective way, that is to say, we must freely decide to appropriate the truth, to make it our own, to the best of our ability. That is what Kierkegaard means when he says "Subjectivity is truth".

It would be a mistake to regard this as declaring his belief in subjectivism, or even in idealism. Other passages of his, might, it is true, send us off on that false scent. He can declare that the thing that really matters is not the object of belief, the *what*, but the manner in which one believes, the *how*. One can pray in truth to God, though worshipping an idol, and one can pray falsely to the true God, thus, in fact, worshipping an idol.[5] But we should not conclude from such statements that the author is indifferent to the object of faith. On the contrary, we shall see that he keeps a firm hold of Christ and the authority of the Bible; he never loses sight of Christ as the sole object of authentic faith. But in the religious domain the truth is accessible only in so far as the person who seeks it commits himself to it, only in so far as he bears witness to it by transforming his own existence so as to correspond with it. In the domain of faith, objectivity is a function of inwardness. "There is a *how*," he writes, "which is always accompanied by its *what*, and that is

5*Ibid.*, 180.

the *how* of faith. Inwardness at its most intense again becomes objectivity."[6]

In fact, the uniqueness of religious truth must be taken into consideration. If I seek God (he says) by the objective way, I shall only arrive at approximations. When I contemplate nature in the hope of finding him, I do, indeed, see omnipotence and wisdom, but I also see much else that disturbs and distresses me. The result is objective uncertainty. I cannot attain to God that way, "because God is a subject, and therefore exists only for subjectivity in inwardness".[7] That does not mean, as some interpreters would have it, that God is only a myth created by our own minds. God is really and truly in creation. "He is in the creation, and present everywhere in it, but directly he is not there; and only when the individual turns to his inner self and hence only in the inwardness of self-activity does he have his attention aroused and is enabled to see God."[8] He who seeks God with the infinite passion of inwardness, that is to say, by prostrating himself before God, in an act of faith and abandonment, he it is who will unfailingly find God. The Eternal is something that can only be obtained in one way. If one is prepared to venture everything for it, one cannot fail to find it. God is precisely that which one takes *à tout prix*.

It is interesting to compare the existential Christianity of Kierkegaard with the atheistic existentialism of Jean-Paul Sartre. For the author of *L'Être et le Néant*,[9] man is essentially desire-to-be-God, a desire doomed to frustration, because his God, the "in-itself" that would, at the same time, be "for-itself" is a contradictory idea. Man is, therefore, a futile being,

---

[6]*Papirer X², A, p. 299; quoted by P. Petit in the preface to his French translation of the Concluding Unscientific Postscript, vii.

[7]*Concluding Unscientific Postscript*, 178.

[8]*Ibid.*, 218.

[9]But see also his self-criticism in *Les Mots*, Paris 1964, 210–11.

a useless passion. Sartre's God is conceived as the sum total of human possibilities. In fact, such a God is self-contradictory and is sought in vain. But the God of Kierkegaard is not the sum of human possibilities; he is the absolute Subject whose existence we attest by staking our all on him. He is only to be found by losing ourselves; but whoever loses himself for God will most certainly discover God, and will rediscover himself too, in God.

What has been said of God here applies also to eternal happiness. We can neither perceive the nature of eternal happiness nor even affirm its reality, if we rely on objective knowledge. Eternal happiness as the absolute good can be defined solely by the way in which it must be acquired. It is the good that can be acquired only by venturing everything absolutely.[10] Its existence can be proved only by the fact that the existent individual himself attests that it exists.[11] And he testifies that it exists when he transforms his life so as to accord with his personal relationship to God and eternal happiness. We have no outward sign of that happiness other than the transformation man's thought effects in man's life. There again, truth resides in inwardness, in the transformation of the subject, effected in his own heart of hearts.

As an example of a thinker who held fast to an objective uncertainty with infinitely passionate inwardness, Kierkegaard mentions Socrates (because, unlike Nietzsche, he admired Socrates in whom he saw a master of the interior life.) Socrates, he says, had no certain, objective proof of immortality, but yet staked his life and risked death for his faith in it. What better proof of immortality could we have?

In the religious domain, therefore, the objective way only

---

[10]*Concluding Unscientific Postscript*, 382 ff.
[11]*Ibid.*, 379.

gives us uncertainty. But it is that very uncertainty that makes possible the infinite passion of which faith consists. Faith, says Kierkegaard, is "an objective uncertainty held fast with the most passionate inwardness".[12] "Without risk there is no faith. Faith is precisely the contradiction between the infinite passion of the individual's inwardness and the objective uncertainty. If I am capable of grasping God objectively, I do not believe; but precisely because I cannot do this, I must believe. If I wish to preserve myself in faith, I must constantly be intent upon holding fast the objective uncertainty, so that in the objective uncertainty I am out 'upon the seventy thousand fathoms of water', and yet believe."[13]

Kierkegaard seems to delight in stressing the irrational element in faith, the idea that its certitude implies a revolt against our intelligence: "Sitting quietly in a ship while the weather is calm is not a picture of faith; but when the ship has sprung a leak, enthusiastically to keep the ship afloat by pumping while yet not seeking the harbour; this is the picture. While intelligence, like a despairing passenger, stretches out its arms towards the shore, but in vain, faith works with all its energy in the depths of the soul; glad and victorious it saves the soul against intelligence."[14]

We shall eventually be forced to conclude that Kierkegaard's Lutheranism made him incapable of doing justice to the eminently rational character of faith. Nevertheless, we must try to grasp what he means. When he talks about objective uncertainty appropriated by the passion of inwardness, he does not mean that faith is a quite arbitrary projection of the aspirations of our own hearts. He means that faith only affirms its object by self-commitment, by a choice or a decision. St

[12]*Ibid.*, 182.
[13]*Ibid.*, 182. Cf. *A Kierkegaard Anthology*, ed. R. Bretall, London 1947, 215.
[14]*Concluding Unscientific Postscript*, 202 note.

Augustine, Pascal, Blondel and many others express more clearly what is fundamentally the same idea when they say that faith is a choice, and depends on our own inward dispositions.

Because there is always an element of uncertainty and conflict in Kierkegaard's concept of faith, it should not be imagined that he conceived it as being a constant prey to doubt. If faith implies conflict, the battle is won, nevertheless, even before battle is joined. In his *On the Concept of Irony* he says: "Faith is combat, and yet it has triumphed over the world before entering the lists. It is in process of becoming what it is. It is not merely a perpetual combat. It is rather a conqueror completing his conquest."[15]

Hitherto we have described faith in terms of subjectivity. Let us now analyse the element of paradox in it.

Undoubtedly, everything we have just said applies in a very special way to Christian faith, but it can apply to other kinds of faith as well, to the faith of Socrates, for example. As soon as the thinking subject conceives an infinite interest in his eternal happiness, faith, or something analogous to it, is his. But Christian faith adds a new and special element. The Christian bases his eternal salvation *on its relation to something that happened in history*, namely, the fact that "God, the Eternal, came into existence in time as a particular man".[16] We are here presented with a twofold paradox: in the first place, eternal happiness is based on a historical event, and in the second place, that historical event—the appearance of the Eternal in time—is a shock to our intelligence. Kierkegaard also distinguishes Christian religiousness from non-Christian religiousness, describing the former as paradoxical religiousness (which he

[15]Quoted by J. Wahl, *Études kierkegaardiennes* (1938), 302.

[16]*Concluding Unscientific Postscript*, 528.

refers to as religiousness B) and the latter as non-paradoxical religiousness (or religiousness A).

In a sense, all faith has a paradoxical quality. "When the eternal truth is related to an existing individual, it becomes a paradox."[17] "The paradoxical character of the truth is its objective uncertainty: this uncertainty is an expression for the passionate inwardness."[18] But instead of finding ourselves confronted with objective uncertainty, as Socrates was with regard to immortality, we can find ourselves faced with the absurd; for the Christian is required to found his eternal salvation on its relation to a historical event, the incarnation of the Eternal, and the Eternal, being outside time, cannot become historical. Here we have the absolute, the supreme, paradox and it shocks and scandalizes us. Now Christian faith consists in freely accepting this paradox, in welcoming it, indeed, with open arms.

Kierkegaard holds forth, with an almost poetic exaltation, on the irrational element in Christianity: the paradox of the incarnation, the paradox of the cross, the paradox of sin. Most of all, he dwells on the incarnation, the divinity of Christ, which is the core of Christianity. He denounces every effort to rationalize it. The paradox of the incarnation, he declares, can be resolved in two ways. It can be treated as an abstract idea, a kind of timeless truth; that is how Hegelianism deals with it. Or it can be put forward, with proofs, as historical; that is what the theologians do. Kierkegaard condemns both the one and the other. He rejects every attempt at rationalization.

For Hegel, he says, the incarnation signifies the concrete unity, the fusion, of the human and the divine in regard to all their potentialities. Christianity is transformed into an eternal history: God in time, a "divine eternal becoming". Jesus' death

[17] *Ibid.*, 187.
[18] *Ibid.*, 183.

has a purely symbolic meaning: it would be merely the out-ward revelation of the most intimate and essential things in all *human* life and history.[19] Hegel tried to reach a synthesis of the eternal and the historical by framing his idea of the eternally historical. Such a play upon words only turns history into myth and theology into anthropology. The logical outcome of Hegelianism is the irreligion of Feuerbach.

For Kierkegaard, however, the incarnation is the unity of God and the man Jesus Christ, who was born, grew up, and lived, in all respects a man, indistinguishable from other men. The *here* and *now* are fundamental. The time of the incarnation is not the historic time; it is the instant that is an atom of eternity. We are faced with the paradoxical, the absurd. But Christianity does not ask to be understood. The nearest we can get to understanding it is to understand that it cannot be under-stood.[20] Christianity is an offence against reason, and it is by way of that offence that we achieve faith.

In Kierkegaard's eyes, the Christian paradox protects both God's transcendence and the personal quality of the object of faith. As to God's transcendence, the paradox is the expression of the infinite distance between man and God—and the only way in which it can be bridged. Hegel, by transforming Christianity into a divinization of humanity, transformed it into its opposite. "All the confusion of modern thought springs from attempting to abolish the qualitative abyss that separates God from man."[21] The paradox re-establishes the infinite distance between them.

[19]Bohlin, quoted by J. Wahl, 128. Wahl adds: "It is right to note, as Bohlin has done, that Hegel strongly insisted on the appearance of the divine in history 'in that man, and that place, and at that particular time', and on the unique and distinctive nature of that manifestation, and on the fact that Hegel chose to contrast Christian *history* with Greek myth."

[20]*Concluding Unscientific Postscript*, 192 ff.

[21]*Journal*, 1847, 222.

The paradox also protects the personal quality of the object of faith. If the appearance of the Eternal in time is essentially paradoxical, it is impossible to treat Christianity as a collection of propositions, a petty system, a philosophy. The object of faith is not a doctrine, it is a person; it is the reality of God in existence; it is Christ as the Man-God.

Moreover, the importance of the teacher is infinitely greater in Christianity than anywhere else. Socrates, when teaching his disciple, was only jogging his disciple's memory. He was only bringing to light something that was already there. Once in possession of the idea, of the doctrine, the disciple could forget all about the teacher. But Christ effects a profound transformation in his disciple, regenerating him and constantly sustaining him in his faith. Christ, therefore, cannot be forgotten. The object of faith is much less Christ's doctrine than Christ's person. Faith is a relationship of one existence to another. It does not correspond at all to the Hegelian caricature of it: it is not "a class for numskulls in the sphere of the intellectual, or an asylum for the feeble-minded". Faith constitutes a sphere all by itself and is distinguished by the infinite interest manifested in the reality of the teacher.[22]

Hegel professed to understand Christianity when he tried to pass it off as "a moment of reflection", a moment of "pure" thought. Kierkegaard rejects this Hegelian effort, which would appear to dissolve the reality of the incarnation into a vague generality. But he also criticizes theologians for insisting on historical proof of Christ's divinity. If the incarnation is not an object of abstract knowledge, neither is it an object of historical knowledge.

We cannot find Christianity by groping through eighteen centuries of past history. Christ is the absolute, and, that being

[22]*Concluding Unscientific Postscript*, 291.

so, we can only attain him in the present. So far as he is concerned, there is only one situation— the contemporary situation. Through faith, we become contemporaries of Christ, we are in the presence of someone of our own time. "From the standpoint of this contemporaneousness, God is no more contemporary with the first Christians than he is with us. In fact, they were his contemporaries not by a direct, historical contemporaneousness, but by a *transhistorical* relationship that is ours as well as theirs."[23]

Only through faith can we reach the Man-God and become his contemporaries. Kierkegaard rejects all pretensions to prove Christianity by its consequences, by its historical fruits. Such an approach could, at the very most, show that Christ was a great man, perhaps the greatest man that ever lived, but not that he was God. That is quite a different matter.[24] History is the sphere of approximations, whereas faith belongs to the sphere of *quality*, attainable only by a leap, the leap of faith.

Again, neither from history nor otherwise, would it be possible to prove the divinity of any man. We should be trying to prove something that was contrary to reason, a pure object of faith. Even the proofs of Christ's divinity given in Holy Writ—his miracles, his resurrection—are objects of faith. Referring to his own miracles, Jesus said: "Blessed is he who takes no offence at me" (*Matt.* 11:67). In these forthright terms he lets us know that there can be no question of proof, so far as he is concerned; that proof can, at most, only excite man's attention, and that, thenceforward, it would be for every man to make up his mind whether he would believe or whether he would take offence. From Christ to us there is no direct communication, that is to say, the Man-God cannot be

[23]J. Wahl, 297.
[24]*Training in Christianity*, 28 ff.

apprehended directly as God.[25] He does not offer us any easy, painless, transition to faith. He confronts us with a choice; we must either believe or be scandalized. Faith is a choice, and the choice we make reveals what is in our hearts.[26]

Confronted with the paradoxical or the absurd, we come back again to subjectivity. Uniting these two elements of paradox and absurdity, Kierkegaard, at the end of his *Concluding Unscientific Postscript* gives this definition of faith: "Faith is the objective uncertainty along with the repulsion of the absurd held fast in the passion of inwardness, which precisely is inwardness potentiated to the highest degree."[27]

Faith, therefore, is not effort to understand; it is the inward transformation of the subject: "One does not prepare oneself to become attentive to Christianity by reading books, or by world-historical surveys, but by immersing oneself deeper in existence".[28]

There, briefly summed up, we have the Kierkegaardian idea of faith. To complete it, we should have to further analyse a number of points only mentioned or implied in what we have said already—points such as the relation of faith to sin and anguish of spirit, various aspects of faith, including faith as love, as grace, as anticipation of eternity, and the completion of faith by imitating Christ. But, in any event, we have sufficiently noticed the most original elements in his conception of faith.

Some of his interpreters have doubted whether Kierkegaard's idea of faith is genuine Christian faith, whether it is not rather a vague spiritual tension not anchored to any object, a vain

[25]Cf. R. Jolivet, *Introduction to Kierkegaard*, tr. W. Barber, London 1950, 182. (Translation of 1946 edn.).

[26]*Training in Christianity*, 32–33, 122.

[27]*Concluding Unscientific Postscript*, 540.

[28]*Ibid.*, 497.

attempt to escape from solitude and nihilism. His God, in that case, would be a myth, a phantom, the offspring of his own subjectivity, nothing masquerading as something. Did he not say himself that he was not a Christian, that he had no faith, that he was only a luckless lover of religion, a plain, ordinary poet with a taste for religious themes?[29]

It is certainly difficult to say whether anyone possesses authentic faith or not. But so far as we are in a position to judge from external evidence, Kierkegaard would seem to have been a genuine Christian. Indeed, he exemplified in himself his own conception of a Christian thinker of the olden days "when a thinker was a believer who strove enthusiastically to understand himself in the existence of faith".[30] Not everyone, of course, who writes religious poetry is necessarily a believer. But when Kierkegaard sees himself as a poet attracted to religious themes, the fact that he does so is evidence of faith. This "luckless lover of religion" perseveres with his unrequited love. And his *Journal* surely is proof enough that he did not merely look at Christianity from the outside and long to go in. Indeed, he lived a Christian life, and by the end of it he had become a sort of saint. When he keeps on saying he is not a Christian, what he has in mind is that there is no such thing as "*being* a Christian"; there is only "*becoming* a Christian". One

---

[29]A. de Waehlens, *La Philosophie de Martin Heidegger*, Louvain 1942, 333-9; Waehlens deals with the much more refined and rather vague statements on this subject in J. Wahl, *Études kierkegaardiennes*, 208, 300-1, 438-45. Cf. R. Vancourt, *Deux conceptions de la philosophie: Husserl et Kierkegaard*, in *Mélanges de Science religieuse*, 1944, 228-9; Merleau-Ponty, "La Querelle de l'existentialisme", *Temps modernes*, novembre 1945, 349; H. de Lubac, *Le Drame de l'humanisme athée*, 1944, 106-7, 112; R. Arnou, *L'Existentialisme à le manière de Kierkegaard, Gregorianum*, 1946, 80; L. Malevez, *Subjectivité et vérité chez Kierkegaard* in *Melanges Marechal*, II, Louvain 1950, 408-23; R. Jolivet, *Kierkegaard*, Paris 1958, 109-21; J. Colette, "Kierkegaard et Lessing", *Revue des Sciences phil. et theol.*, 1960, 20-22.

[30]*Concluding Unscientific Postscript*, 273.

does not *have* Christianity; one just keeps on straining every
nerve to get it—there's the rub! I cannot consider myself a
Christian; all I can do is trust in God that I am. Have I faith?
Kierkegaard asks himself. No, he replies. Does that mean he is
an unbeliever? On the contrary. Faith is, for him, something
one cannot lay claim to; to claim one has it proves that one
has not got it. Faith implies endless choices and decisions, endless struggles for certitude, endless anxiety to know if one has
it. This state of uncertainty is, in fact, a sign of faith. Perhaps
Kierkegaard hoped to hear a voice within him whisper some
day the reassuring words: "Be at peace, dear soul, faith you
have in full measure; if you suffer from anxiety it is because
such suffering is inseparable from inwardness."[31]

Let no one say that his faith was only the tension of his
subjectivity and his God only "a creature of his imagination,
conjured out of the void—nothing tricked out as something".[32]
We must not misunderstand him when he asserts that subjectivity is truth. His meaning, as we have seen, is that faith is
no abstraction; it is the self-commitment of the subject, a
decision, an option. That does not imply by any means that
it has no object at all. On the contrary, in the domain of
religion, objectivity can be attained only through subjectivity.
Without belittling the role of criticism, Kierkegaard believes in
the Bible as the word of God. The object of his faith is Christ,
God made man, God entering time and history. His faith is
directed towards an absolute Other, who is a Person. He could
have taken credit for the saying of a more recent theologian:
"I do not know if I believe, but I do know whom I believe
in".[33]

---

[31]*Journal*, 1845, quoted by J. Wahl, 300.

[32]A de Waehlens, *loc. cit.*, 339.

[33]P. Althaus, *Grundriss der Dogmatik*, 1929, 19, quoted with approval by
K. Barth, *Dogmatik*, 1/1, 1932, 249.

For the believer of our times, in constant grips with atheistic humanism or with the temptation to reduce Christianity to purely earthly perspectives, Kierkegaard could, in certain circumstances, turn out to be a friend. His sense of the Absolute stimulates and purifies faith and prevents it from sinking to the human level. But one could never become a whole-hearted disciple of his. Anyway, he would have been against anything of that kind; like Socrates, his aim was only to awaken minds. His thought is a stimulant, but his point of view is one we could never adopt. While we would never accuse it of being unadulterated solipsism and disguised nihilism (as some have done), we have to conclude, nevertheless, that his Lutheran fideism is not compatible with the Catholic idea of faith.

Christianity, he says, is paradox. In resisting every effort to reduce it to human speculation and to treat it as thought and action at the merely human level, Kierkegaard did well. But the idea of paradox is too exclusively negative. Christianity would mean nothing to us if it did not offer something for the mind to hold on to. We would prefer to think of it as a mystery rather than a paradox. The difference lies in the fact that, if the mystery itself is obscure, it lets some light through to us. As a statement of scientific truth we should find it incomprehensible, but it helps us to understand ourselves; it reveals us to ourselves and gives us a guiding principle for our actions. If Christianity is not purely speculative thought, nevertheless thought is an essential element in it. Faith is more than a decision in a paradoxical situation; it is free adherence of the spirit to the divine Word who communicates himself through the medium of meaningful human words.

Christianity, Kierkegaard maintains, can be proved neither by history not by anything else. It is attained by a "leap", by running the risk of being scandalized. True, when man is brought face to face with signs that announce the Christian message, he may reject it. Faith is an act of obedience, an option that reveals the dispositions of the heart. But it is not a leap in the dark. While no reason for believing dispenses us from believing, yet we do not believe without reason. The life and teaching of Christ and the Church are signs in which the believer actually sees a manifestation of God. One does not believe without perceiving that one can and ought to believe. The option of faith implies an act of apprehension that grounds and justifies it.

What is true of Christian faith is true also, and in an even stricter sense, of simple faith in God. Kierkegaard deems it impossible—indeed ridiculous—to set about proving that God exists: "One proves God's existence by worship, not by proofs".[34] When it comes to affirming the actual existence of the Creator, and not just the unity and absolute nature of the thought, it must surely be admitted that no demonstration will ever convince anyone who is determined to refuse worship. But that does not imply that proof of God's existence is point-less. Such proof serves to express the rational structure of the movement by which the human spirit is induced to worship. Perhaps Kierkegaard saw that this was so. In a little-known passage he writes: "Dialectics is in its truth a benevolent helper, which discovers and assists in finding where the absolute object of faith and worship is . . . Dialectics itself does not see the absolute, but it leads, as it were, the individual up to it, and says: 'Here it must be, that I guarantee; when you worship here, you worship God.' But worship itself is not dialectics."[35] The part played by proof of God's existence seems to be recog-nized here, at least to some extent. Unfortunately, his anti-Hegelian polemics often betrayed the author into refusing to credit Hegelianism with any sense or significance.

[34]*Concluding Unscientific Postscript*, 485.
[35]*Ibid.*, 438–9.

As we have seen, Kierkegaard also denounced the idea of the incarnation which he thought was held by the Hegelians, that is, the fusion of the divine and the human, a "divine eternal becoming"— an evolving Absolute—in history. The incarnation is for him the meeting-point of the Eternal and the historian in the "Instant," that is, at the very moment the individual makes the act of faith that renders him contemporary with it. But in order that the individual may become contemporary with the incarnation otherwise than in an imaginary sense, Christ dead and risen must, in some way, be present in every period of history. And in what other way could he be so if not by his presence in the Church in which he lives? The contemporaneity of faith is only possible in the bosom of the Church which is the body of Christ.

Finally, we have to ask whether Kierkegaard's faith does not isolate the believer from nature and from the community of mankind. The "individual" is alone before God. The religious life separates him alike from natural activity and human intercourse. Hegel could supply the necessary corrective to this point of view by helping to connect faith with history and human society. Christians "have to live the marriage of the holy Spirit and human history that began with the incarnation".[36] That marriage, however, is rendered possible only by conversion. Christianity imposes a vertical transcendence, a death and a resurrection. Kierkegaard, the "knight of faith" deserves a hearing in this connection. If we were to view the convergence of his and Hegel's thought from another angle, we should find that the place at which they intersect—the place that marks the synthesis of subjectivity and objectivity—is identical

---

[36]Merleau-Ponty, "Foi et bonne foi" in *Temps modernes*, fevrier 1946, 776; this article is discussed by Jean Danielou in *Transcendance et Incarnation Dieu vivant*, no. 6. Fr Danielou comes out strongly on the transcendence of Christianity and its relation to the world.

with the Catholic Church. The need for transcendence, affirmed by Kierkegaard, and the need for a historical incarnation, stressed by Hegel, are there reconciled. Through the despair of sin and the hope of resurrection the affirmation of God becomes the affirmation of man, and conversely.

IV

DIALECTICAL THEOLOGY

Dialectical theology was the name given to a school of thought that developed among Protestant theologians after the first World War. Its principal representatives are Karl Barth, Eduard Thurneysen, Friedrich Gogarten, Emil Brunner, and Rudolf Bultmann. The views shared by these theologians were announced to the world in no uncertain manner, all in the course of one year, the year 1921–1922. In that year there appeared Gogarten's *Die religiöse Entscheidung*,[1] Brunner's *Erlebnis, Erkenntnis, und Glaube*,[2] Thurneysen's *Dostoievski*, and the second edition of Barth's *Der Römerbrief* (Commentary on the Epistle to the Romans),[3] and the last-mentioned was the subject of a favourable notice by Bultmann.[4] During the autumn of 1922, Barth, Gogarten and Thurneysen founded the review *Zwischen den Zeiten*, with G. Merz as editor. This was

[1]Jena 1921.
[2]Tübingen 1921.
[3]2nd edn., Munich 1922.
[4]In the review *Christliche Welt* 1922, 320 ff.

to be the organ of their collaboration, and Brunner and Bultmann were early contributors. Before the year was out, someone had labelled the new brand of theological thought "dialectical theology".

We shall see later on that the underlying unity implied by the specific label did not go very deep. Dialectical theology was, indeed, only the prototype of a theology of the Word of God, and, as time went on, it would appear under different aspects. Its earliest characteristic was the energetic reaction of its promoters against the liberal school of theology, of which they had formerly been enthusiastic adherents. Moved, however, by the exigencies of pastoral work and the spiritual crisis provoked by the war, and also by the ideas of Blumhardt, Kutter, Kierkegaard, Overbeck, Dostoevsky and others, they became convinced that liberal theology, centred in religion or piety, and devoted to studying manifestations of these in human psychology or history, had arrived at a point where it was now entirely concerned with man, while still believing it was concerned with God. The members of the new school, therefore, affirmed the transcendence of God in relation to all human knowledge and activity, religion included; they stood for the sovereignty of divine revelation in Jesus Christ, and the authority of the Bible. They recalled that sinful man, even when he believes, always comes before God with empty hands. On this particular point they were at one with the Reformers, but that did not mean they remained adherents of orthodox Protestant theology.

The second edition of Barth's commentary on the Epistle to the Romans is universally considered to be the most vigorous and radical expression of the quality by which their theology merited the appellation "dialectical". We propose, therefore, to deal with this first, and then go on to consider the rest in relation to it.

1. *The Dialectic of Barth*

Dialectic is carried on by a process of negativing, or negation. In the *Römerbrief* this is referred to as *critical negation*. This negation is that which was pronounced by God himself on man in the death and resurrection of Christ. There we find that man has no relationship with God save in so far as God silences him dialectically. It is by passing judgement on us that God pardons us; in the "No" of his anger, we hear the "Yes" of his mercy. All human existence, religion included, is amenable to that divine "No". "The true God, himself removed from all concretion, is the Origin of the *crisis* of every concrete thing, the Judge, the negation of this world" (R 82).[5]

This "critical negation" establishes *distance*. A "barrier of death" divides God from man, time from eternity; Kierkegaard called this an infinite qualitative difference. Moreover, God cannot be contained in religious experience or even in the most stupendous historical happening. In fact, he reveals himself only in Jesus Christ, manifesting himself as the Totally Other, the Unknown God. The Calvinistic notion of *majestas Dei* inspires what Barth borrowed from R. Otto or from the religious philosophy influenced by neo-Kantianism. Even in the most intimate communion between God and man, God is still God, and man but dust and ashes. Their encounter takes place only in the miracle and paradox of faith.

But the cross of Christ throws a bridge over the abyss between God and man at the same time as it deepens that abyss. The critical negation has a *dialectical* quality, that is to say, it includes an affirmation and a return to final unity (R 116). "In Jesus God is known to be the unknown God" (R 114). "As the

[5]Translator's note: The abbreviation (R), followed by a number, refers to the page in the English translation of the 6th edn. of *Der Römerbrief* entitled *The Epistle to the Romans* (tr. E. C. Hoskyns), London 1933.

non-existence of all things, he is their true being" (R 78).
"Every impress of revelation in history . . . is not ex-
tinguished and destroyed as it passes through the judgement,
but is thereby . . . established and confirmed" (R 78). This
dialectical quality is most evident in the dialectic of Adam and
Christ which constitutes both our justification and our resurrection. "The dualism of Adam and Christ, of the old and the
new, is not metaphysical but dialectical. The dualism exists
only in so far as it dissolves itself. It is a dualism of one movement . . . of one road from here to there . . . The *crisis* of
death and resurrection, the *crisis* of faith, is a turning from the
divine 'No' to the divine 'Yes'. There is no subsequent
reverse movement" (R 176–77).

But this turning, this passage, from the divine "No" to the
divine "Yes" has not taken place in human psychology and
history. It is "the absolute act of an invisible occurrence in
God" (R 189). Just as the resurrection of Jesus is not merely
one historical event amongst other events of his life and death,
the new life it introduces into my being is not merely one event
among others in my own life (R 195). The new man that I am
is not what I am. Only by faith am I what I am (and am not)
(R 149). "We can only believe and believe that we believe"
(R 150). This faith is essentially hope, the expectation of
eternity to come (R 317). Inasmuch as it is a human act, it is
but a void (R 57) like the life of Jesus himself (R 30). This non-
historical character of the relationship between God and man
(that is to say, the idea that it does not become effective in the
course of *human* history) is put more clearly by Barth in his
famous passage: "In the resurrection the new world of the
holy Spirit touches the old world of the flesh but touches it as
a tangent touches a circle, that is, without touching it. And
precisely because it does not touch it, it touches it as its frontier
—as the new world" (R 30). The history of salvation is

enacted on the frontier of time and eternity in "the eternal moment" (R 501).

In so far as they are human possibilities, religion and the Church are in the shadow of sin and death; the ethical problem in our case is a deadly disease. Religion, Church, moral action, are only "signs, witnesses, types, recollections, and signposts to the revelation itself, which lies beyond actual reality" (R 129; cf. 444).

Theology is in the same plight. The theologian ought to speak of God; but, being a man, that is something he cannot do. What he says will be no more than "a witness to God's truth" (WT 186, 209).[6] And in order that this may be so, he should preferably employ the dialectical method, which combines in itself both the dogmatic method and the critical, "both (being) referred constantly to their common presupposition, to the living truth which . . . may not be named, but which lies between them and gives their meaning and interpretation to the affirmation and the negation" (WT 206). This living and unutterable truth that lies in the centre, that is to say, the fact that God becomes man, cannot be apprehended or beheld; there can be no direct information about it. "Our task is to interpret the Yes by the No and the No by the Yes without delaying more than a moment on the Yes or the No" (WT 207). But the dialectician must not forget that what he says is based upon "the presupposition of that living original Truth there in the centre" (WT 210).

In 1927, Barth, in his *Die christliche Dogmatik im Entwurf,*[7]

---

[6]Translator's note: The abbreviation (WT), followed by a number, refers to the page in the English translation of *Das Wort Gottes und die Theologie*, Munich 1924 (a collection of articles published between 1916 and 1923); the English title is *The Word of God and the Word of Man* (tr. A. D. Horton), London 1928.

[7]See vol. I: *Die Lehre vom Worte Gottes. Prolegomena zur christliche Dogmatik,* Munich 1927.

again declares, in almost identical terms, that dogmatic thought is a dialectical type of thought, that is to say, a dialogue, proceeding by statement and counter-statement without ever arriving at the last word (pp. 456–62). But he expressly replaces the theme of critical negation by a positive affirmation of God's faithfulness (p. 258). He has given up saying that God is the Totally Other and that faith is a void. He endeavours to introduce revelation into history (pp. 230–32, 239). His *Die kirchliche Dogmatik* will further accentuate this feature; it will lay great emphasis on the Yes that God says to man in Jesus Christ, and it will cease to insist that theology must be dialectical.

2. *The Dialectic of Gogarten, Bultmann and Brunner*

During the period from 1921 to 1924 or thereabouts, Gogarten, Bultmann, and (to a lesser extent perhaps) Brunner, were thinking on remarkably similar lines to Barth, as regards the role attributed to negativity. The idea of God, according to Gogarten, "signifies the absolute crisis of everything human including each and every religion".[8] Bultmann wrote: "God signifies the total suppression, the repudiation, of man, the challenging of man's right to exist, the pronouncing of judgement on man".[9] And Brunner: "It is only at the crisis, at the point where man is approaching his end, that God's grace can intervene as grace".[10] All three hold that revelation and faith transcend historical knowledge and religious experience; God reveals himself in Jesus Christ as the Totally Other, and pronounces a radical No accompanied by an original and final Yes; man, though justified, remains a sinner and can only pin his faith on divine forgiveness. But we do not find any of the

---

[8] *Die religiöse Entscheidung*, 3.
[9] *Glauben und Verstehen*, I, Tubingen 1933, 18.
[10] *Die Mystik und das Wort* (2nd edn.), Tübingen 1928, 298–9.

three holding, as Barth did, that the fundamental opposition of time and eternity constitutes a barrier between *two* worlds; they hold that the barrier divides our own world. The dialectic, the crisis, is not, as in Barth's *Römerbrief*, "the absolute act of an invisible occurrence in God". The instant at which it takes place is not the eternal moment beyond the confines of time, but the precisely determined instant when the Word of God incarnate encounters the human decision which is faith. True, this divergence from Barth's view is hardly perceptible, all the less so as Barth and the others all affirm that divine revelation is the reply to the question of human existence.

In order to give themselves room to manoeuvre, so to speak, when dealing with the human decision involved by faith, Gogarten, Bultmann and Brunner, from 1926 onwards, proceeded to incorporate, as a postulate, with their theology, the understanding that man has of himself. It then became apparent that their conception of dialectical theology was quite different from that of Barth.

According to Gogarten,[11] the reason why all discussion about God is dialectical, is that we have no knowledge of him which is not at the same time, and primarily, knowledge of ourselves. It is not our relationship to God but our existence that is dialectical. The duality of the Creator and the creature does away with the possibility of a dialectical relationship, because it rules out all unity, all relative exchange, between the two elements. There is only a dialectic of the creature, a dialectic that takes place within historic time, inasmuch as my present decision assumes my perishable past and so confers on it an imperishable quality. Gogarten then goes on to explain that the constitutive element of history is faith in creation, the content of that faith being the encounter with the concrete

[11]In *Ich glaube an den dreieinigen Gott*, Jena 1926.

thou, the response to the presence of one's neighbour. His later work aimed at basing the relations between the individual and society on the I-thou relationship, the analysis of which he borrowed from F. Ebner and M. Buber.

Bultmann, too, declares that theology cannot speak of God without at the same time speaking of man; consequently it presupposes, when it speaks, a determinate conception of man. After 1928, or so, he borrowed the idea of "precomprehension" from Heidegger: man's being is historical, that is to say, it is a possibility; it is constantly at work in the concrete circumstances of life; it is subject to decisions in which man chooses himself as *his* possibility.[12] "Dialectical theology" is now defined by Bultmann as the consciousness of man's historicity and of the historicity of human discussion about God.[13] The proposition "God forgives me" is dialectical, not in the sense that it would be completed and made explicit by the mention of its correlative—God's anger towards the sinner (which is in itself explicit)—but inasmuch as it is historical, inasmuch as it is a statement of the action of God's forgiveness.[14]

The kind of self-knowledge postulated in the dialectical theology peculiar to the trio of theologians under review is the knowledge of self that the non-believer can attain. According to Brunner, this self-knowledge constitues the contact-point of divine revelation with the human intelligence. Wholly sinful but not thereby ceasing to be God's image in the formal sense, man is a contradiction. That is why the divine message is at once an aggesssive challenge to man as well as man's perfection and fulfilment. That is also why theology must be dialectical. The word "dialectical" could indeed be rendered by "reflecting contradiction". Because the Word of God

[12]*Glauben und Verstehen*, I, 118.
[13]*Glauben und Verstehen*, I, 118.
[14]*Loc. cit.*, 117.

encounters man "in contradiction", it is itself "in contradiction". It uses terms such as Man–God, foolish wisdom, liberty in the service of God, and the like. It is in paradox, indeed, that it is most fittingly expressed.[15]

And so, despite the shades of difference in their views, Brunner, Bultmann and Gogarten are all of the opinion that the dialectical nature of theology is based on the dialectic of human existence (and not on the negativing action of revelation). Barth reproaches them for admitting, side by side with the Word of God, a second sovereign court of appeal.[16] He holds that human existence can only be considered in the light of the Word of God and he deliberately annuls everything in his earlier writings that could give rise to the impression that theology rests on a philosophical analysis of existence.[17] He no longer contends that divine revelation is a reply to the question of human existence.

When Gogarten, in 1933, announced his adherence to the "German Christian" school, Barth, in turn, announced the severance of his own connection with the review *Zwischen den Zeiten*, whose editor thereupon wound up that enterprise. The following year Barth vigorously repudiated the "natural theology" whose claims were being pressed by Brunner. Thenceforward each of the members of the quondam quartet has followed his own bent. And the mainspring of their thought has ceased to be that "critical negation" which first brought them together.[18]

[15]*Zwischen den Zeiten*, 1929, 265–6.
[16]*Ibid.*, 1933, 297–314.
[17]*Kirchliche Dogmatik*, I, 1, viii, 128–135.
[18]All contemporary dialogue with these writers should, therefore, be oriented, preferably, towards their later work. No useful purpose is served by discussing ideas or formulae which they have themselves modified or tacitly relinquished. This is especially relevant in the case of Barth, who has modified his early ideas much more than Brunner and Bultmann.

V

THE PROBLEM OF NATURAL THEOLOGY AS SEEN BY K. BARTH AND R. BULTMANN

The First Vatican Council teaches that God, the beginning and end of all things, may be certainly known by the natural light of human reason, by means of created things.[1] Catholic philosophers evolve rational proofs of the existence of God and believe they can, independently of divine revelation, throw some light on the relation of man and the world to him. Theologians and apologists regard these items of knowledge as "preliminaries to faith"—and indeed, as the very bed-rock of dogmatics.

The Protestant theologians Karl Barth, Emil Brunner and Rudolf Bultmann have discussed this doctrinal ensemble and rejected it. It is important to be quite clear on their motive for doing so.

When philosophers contest the validity of natural theology,

---

[1]Denzinger, no. 1 785.

they do so on epistemological or ontological grounds. If they declare the idea illusory, it is because they believe they can detect paralogisms in it. But the trio of Protestant theologians we have mentioned are animated by an entirely different motive. They challenge it in the name of the Word of God attested in the Bible; they hold that the Word of God condemns natural theology as idolatrous.

True, their argument is not wholly devoid of traces of philosophical criticism. Having spent their student-years in an atmosphere of neo-Kantianism, they could hardly help imbibing the conviction that all philosophical proofs of God's existence are vain. But this, they assert, is not the primary reason why they reject such proofs. They condemn natural theology, because the Bible, they say, rejects, as an idolatrous image, every god other than the God of revelation, and declares that there is no access to the true God except by way of faith in his Word.

This doctrine, they hold, figures even in the very texts where Catholic tradition professes to find support for the fact, or the possibility, of a natural knowledge of God—for example, in St Paul's discourse in the Areopagus (*Acts* 17:22 ff.), or better still, in the first chapter of the Epistle to the Romans. They admit the apostle recognizes that God reveals himself in creation, and that a natural knowledge of God is, therefore, a possibility. They point, however, to St Paul's statement in the same context, that the pagans have never actualized, and indeed are incapable of actualizing, this possibility. The reason St Paul mentions the matter is not to invite the pagans to develop a valid natural theology but to denounce their idolatry as in-excusable, and to invite them to believe in God, who is revealed in Jesus Christ.

And so, in the name of Holy Writ, Barth, Brunner and Bultmann refuse to accept the natural theology evolved in the

Catholic Church. All pretensions to know God by the light of human reason, independently of biblical revelation, can only result in a false god. On that point the trio of Protestant theologians are agreed.

But, while they are agreed on that point, there are other points on which they differ notably among themselves. Brunner and Bultmann think that the Christian message can and should find a point of contact either in the non-Christian religions or in philosophy. In their eyes, indeed, man, though a sinner, retains an essential relation to God; consciously or unconsciously he is concerned with the idea of God. In so far as he is content to confine himself to what he can discover unaided, he has only a perverted knowledge. But the preacher of the Christian message who would confute this perverted knowledge can, and should, start from the essential God-man relationship or the question that lies at the root of it, if he wants to guide the non-Christian towards the faith. The theologian, too, if he would build his science on a sure basis, can, and should, make the faith his point of departure and then go on to explain this relationship or question that is immanent in every man. All this will result in something that will still merit the description "natural theology". It will be quite different, though, from what Catholicism understands by that term, because it would have taken the Christian faith as its starting-point and developed its argument in the light and in the bosom of the faith. This is not at all the same as the spontaneous, independent development of a natural knowledge of God obtained by man's reason alone. It is, in fact, the theological interpretation of natural revelation or of the problem of God. It has the advantage, they say, that it permits of dialogue with the non-believer, who, on his side, starts from the standpoint of his religion or his philosophy or his conception of man.

These views provoked an energetic protest from Barth, and

led to his estrangement from his friends and associates. The Christian revelation for him was not the reply to a question posed by man as such; it has no point of contact with man. It is the Christian revelation itself that raises the question and creates the point of contact. If there is anything that can be called a natural revelation, it is not distinct from the action of Christ; it is not known otherwise than in Jesus Christ.

Let us now consider Barth's thesis in more detail. When we have done that, we can go back to Bultmann.

1. The Thesis of Karl Barth

Barth's views are expressed in a passage of exceptional vigour in the Commentary on the Apostles' Creed which appeared in 1935 under the title Credo:

> "God" in the meaning of the symbol—of the symbol which aims at giving again the testimony of the prophets and apostles—"God" is not a magnitude, with which the believer is already acquainted before he is a believer, so that as believer he merely experiences an improvement and enrichment of knowledge that he already had. When Paul says (Rom. 1:19) that what can be known of God is manifest to them, for God manifested it unto them, the whole context as well as the immediately preceding statement (Rom. 1:18) shows that Paul sees the truth about God "held down" among men, made ineffective, unfruitful. What comes of it in their hands is idolatry. And with Paul, as with all the prophets and apostles, idolatry is not a preparatory form of the service of the true God, but its perversion into the very opposite, to which, therefore, they, with their witness to God, do not attach but oppose their witness . . . The word "God" in the symbol, therefore, must not mislead us into first giving considera-

tion to the nature and attributes of a being which, on the basis of our most comprehensive experiences and deepest reflection, we think we have discovered as that which this name may and must fit, in order, thereupon, under the guidance of the historical statements of the symbol, to ascribe to the subject so conceived this and that definite predicate, behaviour and act. On the contrary, we have to begin with the admission that of ourselves we do *not* know what we say when we say "God", i.e. that all that we think we know when we say "God" does not reach and comprehend him who is called "God" in the symbol, but always one of our self-conceived and self-made idols, whether it is "spirit" or "nature", "fate" or "idea" that we really have in view. But even this admission, of course, cannot carry the meaning that in it we are proclaiming a discovery of our own . . . Only God's revelation, not our reason despairing of itself, can carry us over from God's incomprehensibility.[2]

If God had not become man, as is recognized and confessed in the second article (of the Creed), then everything we could conceive and say to ourselves about God *over* man and about God *with* man, would hang in the air as arbitrarily, as mistakenly and as misleadingly, as the corresponding ideas which in the long run have been fashioned about God and man in all religions and cosmic speculations.[3]

Barth, it is true, has not always displayed such a negative attitude with respect to the natural knowledge of God. In the celebrated Commentary on the Epistle to the Romans (1922), or in the lectures delivered by him about the same time,

[2]*Credo* (tr. J. S. McNab), London 1936, 11–12.
[3]*Ibid.* 40.

certain statements—as he himself afterwards acknowledged—
were derived from natural theology. The natural theology had
not, so to speak, come in by the main gate, but it had slipped
in somehow. Nothing could be farther from his mind than
to put forward proof of the existence of God. But he admitted
that from all religions an appealing cry goes up to Jesus Christ,
and, moreover, that there is an actual encounter between the
Christian revelation and Plato-inspired philosophy. Plato, he
said, bore witness to the "Totally-Other"—the transcendent
God—and by doing so may be said to have announced the
revelation of God in Jesus Christ.[4]

A few years later, in 1929, Barth simultaneously shed the
concept of the "Totally-Other" and any vestiges of natural
theology he may have hitherto harboured. Thenceforward the
tone of his polemics becomes shriller. He denounces the "so-
called knowledge of God" affirmed by the First Vatican
Council, and refers to the *analogia entis* as "the invention of
Antichrist".[5] In 1933, he broke with his friends, whose views
were less radical than his own.[6] Brunner, having tried to
resume dialogue with him by drawing up a careful synopsis of
"a Christian natural theology", provoked Barth to reply with
his famous tract "No!" (1934).[7] Written in anger, this is too
one-sided to give an accurate idea of what was in Barth's mind.
To get that we must read the more coherent and complete
account in the volume of the *Dogmatik* which treats *ex professo*
of the knowledge of God (1940).

The volume devoted to anthropology (1950) marks the
first appearance of a certain flexibility in Barth's thought. He
brings himself to acknowledge that philosophers who reflect

[4]See *Karl Barth*, I, 138–39.
[5]*Kirchliche Dogmatik*, I, 1. Preface.
[6]See *Karl Barth*, I, 206–11.
[7]*Ibid.* I, 211–19.

upon God may have something worthwhile to say; here he had Jaspers particularly in mind. He admits, too, that Brunner's line of thought is quite legitimate—at any rate up to a point. He shows himself more receptive to the idea of a manifestation of God in creation.[8] In the latest volumes of the *Dogmatik*, no more polemics are hurled against the analogy of being. But, these signs of appeasement notwithstanding, he persists in his condemnation of natural theology.

To understand the cause and effect of this condemnation we must go, in the first place, to the chapter of the *Dogmatik* that deals with the knowledge of God.

1. According to the Bible, Barth says, the true God, Father, Son and holy Spirit, Creator, Reconciler and Redeemer, can be known by us only through the grace of revelation, in Jesus Christ and with the help of the holy Spirit. And the power of knowing God belongs to man not in virtue of what he is in himself, but because he exists in Jesus Christ. These two theses, argued at considerable length,[9] rule out right away (so Barth says) all possibility of a natural knowledge of the true God, even before the question is raised. If it has to be raised at all, the object should not be to discuss it but simply to allow it to sink into our heart of hearts when we realize that the Word of God has spoken for us also.

2. That this is so (the author goes on to say) is apparent even from the many biblical texts which, on first reading, would seem to point to the possibility of attaining a knowledge of God independently of divine revelation. As a matter of fact, when the Bible says that pagans have a natural knowledge of God, it is far from implying that they had acquired, or could acquire, any such knowledge by their own efforts. No, the Bible roundly declares that they have made the truth prisoner

[8] *Ibid.* III, 130–32.
[9] *Ibid.* III, 77–92.

of their idolatry. The knowledge it attributes to the pagans is an "imputed" knowledge that belongs "objectively" to their being in Christ, but is "subjectively" still foreign to their minds.

Here, for example, is how Barth interprets the first chapter of the epistle to the Romans:

> The same Calvary which showed that the Jews never observed their own Law, also made it clear that the pagans, too, kept sinning against God and bore no less responsibility. Yes, the pagans sinned against the truth, which was well-known even to them. God had always been manifest to them. The world round about them had never ceased to be his creation; it bore witness to his activity, and, therefore, to himself. Though they refused to give honour and thanks to God, though they had sunk into the void, the darkness, and the folly of idolatry, they always remained, objectively speaking, beings that were acquainted with God. Even when they denied and betrayed the truth, they were always, objectively, in a positive relationship with it. And so they, too, had no excuse . . . They, too, must acknowledge that God's anger was justly visited upon them . . . Mark it well: all this is no catechism compiled from pagan sources, no inheritance of traditional knowledge brought with them when they received the gospel message, no result of their own reflection, for such reflection was entirely beyond their powers. Far from it! All this is strange news for the pagans; this is something they have never heard before. And equally strange news for the Jews is the judgement pronounced upon them—the Chosen People—in the divine revelation, the judgement that says they have always been transgressors of the Law. And knowledge of all this

is attributed (*zugeschrieben, zugerechnet, imputiert*) to the pagans as the truth about themselves . . . It is not by any means a vague, general, abstract truth with no foothold in historic time; indeed it cannot be disconnected for a single moment from the apostolic message and made into a thesis on anthropology or religious philosophy or apologetics. It is the dark side, the "judgement" (*Gericht*) side of the gospel preached to the pagans. It is the objective sentence (*Urteil*) pronounced on man and is founded on the message of Jesus Christ who was rejected by the Jews, who was crucified and rose on the third day from the dead; for Jesus Christ revealed the truth about God and the truth about man, and the truth about man is that man belongs to God . . . How, then, could anybody extract from this text a vague, general, abstract, timeless truth to the effect that man acquires by himself and in his own right as man, a natural knowledge of God? . . . Paul treats man in the cosmos as a witness—an *involuntary* witness, mark you!—of revelation. He goes farther than that . . . He treats man with the utmost, the most remorseless seriousness; he speaks to him in the most concrete language; but the seriousness and the con-creteness . . . lie in the fact that God's revelation, whose signs can be read by man in the cosmos, is *introduced* into the cosmos by the God-given power of God's own prophets and apostles. Here Paul establishes what we may call contact (*Anknüpfung*) between the Christian message and non-Christian man. But we can only call it that if we bear in mind that the point of contact (*Anknüpfungspunkt*) in man's case is not posited already (before the gospel message has reached him), but is *posited anew* in and with the preaching of the gospel.[10]

[10]*Kirchliche Dogmatik*, II, 1, 133–34.

The train of thought that runs through this Commentary and other analogous works of Barth can be summed up as follows. Every man, inasmuch as he has been created in Jesus Christ and continues to exist in Jesus Christ, is capable of attaining to knowledge of God. But, being essentially a sinner, he is cut off from direct access to the true God. It is only by Christ's grace that he has power to know God, and it is only by faith in Christ that he can realize this power in action.

That is why the claim to be able to know God by the un-aided human reason constitues—in Barth's words—"an outrage upon the Christian idea of God".[11]

3. How it is, then, that natural theology keeps on cropping up regularly in Christian theology, and even in specifically Protestant theology? Barth accounts for this by saying that the vitality of natural theology is the vitality of man himself.[12] Human nature, even in the Christian, is engaged in a perpetual struggle with grace, and its apparent disposition to receive grace is, in effect, a disposition to resist it. An ineluctable impulse urges man's nature to assert itself, to understand itself, and to justify itself. The effort to do so necessarily leads it to declare that it can acquire knowledge of God without the help of God's grace. In trying to solve, by its own efforts, the enigma of its existence and the riddle of the universe, it discerns, at the beginning and at the end of its efforts, a principle and an object, respectively, which it thinks is God. Even before this natural theology becomes explicit, human nature already puts it into practice in its own free actions. It would deny its own existence if it did not do so.

And so we find that the very thing which explains the vitality of natural theology is the very thing that rules it out as

[11]*Ibid.* II, I. 140.

[12]*Ibid.* II, I. 185.

illegitimate, i.e. the fact that it originates in the free act of sinful man.

4. We can see that the possibility of a natural knowledge of the true God is not rejected by Barth out of agnosticism or on epistemological grounds; he rejects it on the ground of biblical revelation. Why, he asks, should not success attend man's effort to solve unaided the enigma of his existence and to discover its first principle and ultimate object? Man could certainly do so. Our whole existence bears witness to that. We can know God. But, from the biblical point of view, such a "God" would be an idol. And that means that every idea conceived and claimed to be an idea of God, is a false god, not because of the idea itself, but because of the claim made for it. Even the "pure" idea of a Plato is no exception to this; indeed it is all the more dangerous because it is pure.[13]

Outside of revelation, what we call our knowledge of God could well be only the projection of man—of man the sinner— on to the plane of the infinite and the absolute. Barth illustrates this with examples drawn from modern philosophy or theology; Kant, Hegel, Schleiermacher, Ritschl, these have all spoken compellingly of God (he says); but, while they may have thought they were doing so, they were, in fact, only speaking about man, about what constitutes the background of man's reason or his religious consciousness. Here Barth's view coincides with that of Feuerbach (to whom indeed, he refers): "Theology is anthropology, in the sense that the object of worship that we call God represents nothing more than man's own nature and being".[14] We may be sure Barth does not take this judgement of Feuerbach's to be the last word in this matter, and, in so far as he accepts it, his reasons are not the

[13]*Ibid.* I, 1. 412.
[14]L. Feuerbach, *Das Wesen der Religion*, 1848, 3rd. lecture; quoted in *Kirchliche Dogmatik*, II, 1. 328.

same as Feuerbach's. But he perceives the challenge it presents
to theologians and thinks that none of them can meet it if they
persist in claiming that knowledge of God is to be got otherwise than through divine revelation.[15]

5. By his refusal to have anything to do with natural theology
(except to condemn it), Barth would radicalize the doctrine of
the Reformers. As he has said himself over and over again,
the Reformers never absolutely condemned all natural
knowledge of God. They waged war against "justification by
works" in the moral sphere, and conducted a similar campaign
in the intellectual sphere, but did not press it quite so hard.
But they did not go so far as to declare that the biblical principle and the principle of justification by faith alone, excluded
all natural theology. In that, says Barth, they were inconsistent.
Today, in order to remain faithful to their principles, they
would have to take the final step and declare plainly that a
natural knowledge of the true God is impossible, because man,
being essentially a sinner, is incapable of co-operating in his
own justification, and because his relationship with God is the
work of God and God alone.

6. In the course of his inquiry, Barth could not fail to come
across the definition of the First Vatican Council with regard
to the natural knowledge of God. He saw very well that it was
"circumspect" and only affirmed a possibility. Nevertheless,
he brought two charges against it. On the one hand, he said,
it splits up the idea of God, as if it were possible to consider
the Creator without, at the same time, envisaging the
Redeemer. On the other hand, and more seriously, it takes no
account of God in his work of revelation but conceives him as
a general type of Supreme Being, with a nature akin to our
own and to that of every other existent being, and identifies

[15]See *Karl Barth*, III, 95–96.

the Lord of the Church with that idol, which is a product of the thought of Aristotle and the Stoics.[16]

7. Barth elsewhere comes across "proofs" of the existence of God. In his opinion, all philosophical proof of God is illegitimate, not—as many nineteenth-century Protestants believed—because of the criticism Kant had levelled against it, but because we pin our faith on the proof God gives us of himself in his own Word, and, therefore, have no need of man-made proofs.

"I have no intention," he says, "of waging war on these 'proofs' of God. I don't know whether they strike you straight away as very delicate and rather comical contrivances. Perhaps they would hold good for the 'gods' so-called. If I wanted to discuss these 'Supreme Beings' with you, I would concentrate on the five so-called proofs of God. The Bible never uses the kind of argument we find there; it simply speaks of God as of him who has no need of proof. It speaks of a God who *proves himself* at every step; here I am, God says, and because I am, live and act, what need is there to prove me? This proof that God gives us of himself is the proof referred to by the prophets and apostles. How can we speak otherwise of God in the Church? God has no need of our proofs."[17]

And so, Barth rejects philosophical proofs because they disregard divine initiative. The most he will concede is that a philosophy such as that of Jaspers *envisages* access to God; but he hastens to add that it does not *give* access to God. On the other hand, however, he allows the legitimacy of a theological proof that would confine itself to reiterating the proof that God gives of himself in biblical revelation. God, he says, exercises his liberty, that is to say, his *aseity*, in the choice and

[16]I have discussed these charges in *Karl Barth*, III, 107-112.

[17]*Dogmatik im Grundriss*, 1947, 42-43.

in the government of Israel, in the incarnation, in the out-
pouring of the holy Spirit. By this active attestation, he proves
his own existence in the midst of the reality that is distinct from
him. The existence of God differs from all other existences
precisely because it begins with itself, because it is *a se*. Consequently, any *human* proof of God's existence, if it is really
to prove his existence, and not an existence other than his,
can only *repeat* the proof God gives of himself in the exercise
of his initiative in revelation.[18]

One proof, Barth adds, fulfils this condition and is of un-
equalled value on that account; it is what has been wrongly
described as the "ontological" proof; it is a proof that has been
constantly misinterpreted—the proof given by St Anselm of
Canterbury in the *Proslogion*. Anselm "proved the existence of
God by stating that God has proved himself, proves himself
and will continue to prove himself, in postulating himself . . .
as the beginning beyond which human thought cannot go,
the beginning with which all thought must begin, because
God, in proving himself, is he *quo maius cogitari nequit:* he whose
holy name excludes not only non-existence, but the very idea
of his non-existence, because the offence of denying his existence is forbidden to man by the fact that God has given himself to man as an object of man's knowledge, and has, at the
same time, given man the light by which that object may be
clearly seen".[19]

Barth, therefore, treats the celebrated text of the *Proslogion*
as a theological proof and not a philosophical one. Anselm, he
says, regards the existence of God as a truth that he would not
for a moment think of questioning; he makes it his starting-
point, treating it as an unassailable presupposition. He has no
intention of proving *that* God exists; but, presupposing that

[18]*Kirchliche Dogmatik*, II, 1. 342–43.
[19]*Ibid.* II, 1. 343.

this affirmation is true, he endeavours to understand and demonstrate *how* it is true. And his understanding of it constitutes the very core of his faith.

We cannot here go into the minute commentary Barth has devoted to this proof.[20] We can only point out its importance. The author declares, in effect, that his radical stand on the question of the knowledge and existence of God is derived from St Anselm, from the *Proslogion*, in particular.[21]

2. Bultmann's Thesis

Bultmann, as we have already seen, is just as strongly opposed as Barth to the natural theology adopted by the Catholic Church, that is, a rational knowledge of God, independent of faith and capable of serving as a foundation for dogmatic theology. Unlike Barth, however, he holds that dogmatic theology must include, as a legitimate and necessary constituent, a natural theology that shall interpret, from the Christian point of view, how "natural" human existence regards its relation to the problem of God.[22]

He begins with what he thinks is the fundamental problem: the understanding of the Word of God attested in the Bible. Now all interpretation, says Bultmann, including that of the Bible, requires that the interpreter shall have experienced, shall have "lived", so to speak, the subject-matter of the text. Such previous experience—or *precomprehension* (*Vorverstandnis*)—of what is discussed in the text will, of course, lend strength to the interpretation. But Bultmann says this theory

[20]*Fides quaerens intellectum. Anselms Beweis der Existenz Gottes,* 1931. We have analysed and discussed this commentary in *Karl Barth,* III, 143–70 and in a communication we sent to the Congress *anselmien du Bec* (*Spicilegium Beccense,* I, 191–207).

[21]*Kirchliche Dogmatik,* II, 1. 2.

[22]See *Karl Barth* I, 198–203 and III, 55–61 for a fuller account of Bultmann's views on this point.

of his has given rise to an objection from a certain source. (Barth is not named, but the objection is obviously his.) The objection contends that there cannot be any precomprehension of what the Bible tells us, because the Bible recounts God's own action; "natural" man has no preliminary relationship with God, and can have no knowledge of God except through revelation, that is to say, through God's own action. Bultmann describes this as a specious objection. True, man cannot have any precomprehension of the divine action in so far as the latter is actualized in an event. That holds good for every event as such. I can know nothing of the death of Socrates or the murder of Caesar before it has been brought, somehow or other, to my notice. But, in order to be able to understand them as historical events, and not as merely unremarkable facts, I must have a precomprehension of the historical possibili-ties in which they acquire their significance and scope; I must know, for instance, what a life means in the philosophical sense, what transforms a fact into a political event, and so on. Similarly, in order to understand accounts of events that are presented as actions of God, I must have a precomprehension of what "action of God" really means. And, if it is objected that, before divine revelation, man can neither know who God is nor what "action of God" signifies, my reply will be simply that man can know quite well who God is. Man's life, as a matter of fact, is affected, consciously or unconsciously, by this question of God. In the classical words of St Augustine: "Tu fecisti nos ad te, et cor nostrum inquietum est donec requiescat in te". If this were not so, it would be impossible for man to recognize God as God, even in God's own revelation. Every human being possesses an existential knowledge of God in the shape of a problem that can masquerade in many different disguises, such as the problem of happiness, of salvation, of the meaning of history, of authenticity. Even if one's faith in a divine revelation only went so far as to feel justified in regarding the problems we have just mentioned as problems of God's existence, that would, in fact, constitute a precomprehension of revelation.[23]

Bultmann, therefore, meets Barth's objection by saying that every man has a knowledge of God, thanks to which the biblical message can be recognized as the Word of God. This knowledge, which is also to be found in non-Christian religions, offers a point of contact for the missionary's preaching; it is also the theologian's ultimate justification for using philosophy in the systematic interpretation of Holy Writ.[24]

Bultmann, however, goes on to say that this knowledge of God is not knowledge of God himself. It is primarily knowledge of man; it is man's consciousness of his own limitations. God appears simply as the power that breaks through the human barriers and thereby raises man to his true stature. Our idea of God is a negative, and not a positive, one. It is nothing more than the *question* of God.

The Christian faith affirms that the sole answer to this question is the Christian answer, and that every other pretended answer is illusive. There is no divine revelation outside of the Christian revelation, and no knowledge of God outside of faith in his Word.

When the apostle Paul refers to natural revelation he has no intention of inviting man to work out a natural theology for himself; he wants to open man's eyes to the revelation of God in Jesus Christ. Natural revelation only makes man aware of his limitations. If he stops short at that, he makes the mistake

---

[23]*Das Problem der Hermeneutik* in *Glauben und Verstehen*, II, 231–32.

[24]See *Das Problem der "naturlichen Theologie"* in *Glauben und Verstehen*, I, 294–332.

of transforming his negative knowledge into a positive knowledge that is misconceived, and God's creation has no further message for him.

That, in Bultmann's opinion, is why natural theology in the Catholic tradition must be regarded as impossible.[25]

3. A Critical Examination

Bultmann, therefore, would seem to reject the Catholic conception of natural theology as whole-heartedly as Barth. Yet it is quite clear that his thesis, more subtle and refined than Barth's, is less removed from the Catholic point of view. We could even acquiesce in the arguments he uses against Barth. They may not, indeed, go far enough, but at least they do deal with some essential points.

To respond effectively to the challenge of these two Protestant theologians, the first thing we must do is to examine the radical position adopted by Barth.

But how are we to deal with this? We could, of course, confute the Barthian doctrine by setting out fully and fairly the teaching common to Catholic theologians and philosophers, making the most of its internal logic and its rational basis. We might confute, but not convince, for the result might be a monologue that would have no impression on those we hoped to persuade. We must rather adopt an attitude of dialogue, starting from the presuppositions of the interlocutor, which may, on examination, reveal rather different implications from those he is aware of.

Before we begin to discuss the fundamental differences that divide us, let us both decide what points we really agree upon in spite of appearances to the contrary. In general, it will be

[25]See *Die Frage der naturlichen Offenbarung* in *Glauben und Verstehen*, II, 79–104 and also *Anknüpfung und Widerspruch* in the same volume, 117–32.

better not to reply to an extreme statement by another extreme statement. Catholic tradition is much more complex and more subtle than would appear from the statements of Barth, Bultmann and their disciples. They have not taken sufficient note that it has already, on its own initiative, done justice to some of the claims they make. It would be wrong if we, too, were to lose sight of this.

Catholic doctrine holds that man can arrive at knowledge of God by the natural light of reason. But it also holds that, in our sinful, human condition, this basic power is, in fact, unlikely to be exercised in an entirely satisfactory manner except under the aegis of the Christian revelation. This is the teaching of the First Vatican Council, and it did no more than sanction a long tradition, based on Holy Writ. Even when Catholic theology showed itself most receptive to the teaching of the pagan philosophers, it only took from them what appeared to accord with the teaching of the Bible. It always resisted every pretension that a natural knowledge of God sufficed for man. In its eyes, refusal to accept the revelation propounded by the Church involves not only limitation of the knowledge of God, but its falsification.[26]

Barth probably knows well enough how near Catholic doctrine is to his own in this matter. He does not appear, however, to have given this sufficient attention. Had he done so, his condemnation would, no doubt, have been hedged about with qualifications—although basically, perhaps, it would not have changed. We can see why. What he considers illegitimate is not just this or that form of natural theology or this or that way in which it might be misused; he repudiates the very idea that a natural knowledge of the true God could be possible. It is at this point precisely that he parts company with Catholic doctrine.

[26]See the texts quoted in *Karl Barth*, III, 98–100.

To inaugurate a genuine dialogue on this particular point,
we must recall that Barth rejects the possibility of such
knowledge not on philosophical grounds, but on the ground
that it is counter to biblical revelation and to faith in Christ.
This, then, must be the point of view from which we examine
his thesis. Two questions arise here. Can we accept his interpretation of the New Testament texts? Can we rule out the
possibility of a natural knowledge of God without, at the same
time, ruling out the possibility of knowledge of faith?

1. Let us take the second question first. Barth states that
knowledge of God by faith presupposes the operation, the
event, of divine grace, that is, the free revelation of God in
Jesus Christ and the free action of the holy Spirit in the believer.
We agree. We would add, however, that knowledge by faith
also presupposes natural knowledge of God. The condition is
not one of chronological anteriority; it is one of the intellectual
order. We say that faith implies *a priori* a pre-existing apprehension of God in the subject; it need not be mentally formulated, but it must be capable of formulation.

In fact, as Barth has very justly remarked, God does not
reveal himself in an immediate and direct manner, but through
created signs, through his special works—the history of Israel
and the human reality of Jesus Christ. Inevitably the question
flashes across our minds: How could the prophets and apostles,
how could we ourselves, recognize the manifestation of God
in these "special works"? Certainly the history of Israel, the
human reality of Jesus, and the Bible that tells us about them,
are striking enough in their originality to compel the attention
of an uncommitted mind. But this originality makes its
appearance in the midst of our own world, these realities are
inserted in our universe and are homogeneous with it. How
could we discern the action of God in them if our spiritual
being did not possess the power of knowing God, if the

Absolute, whose presence is perceptible in our heart of hearts, bore no relation to the God of whom the Bible speaks? We can hardly appeal to a miracle of revelation or of grace that takes hold of, and subjugates, our spirit. This would, in turn, provoke another question. How can we know that our faith is, in fact, the result of a miracle, that is to say, of an action of God, rather than that of an arbitrary human decision? Unless we had a pre-existing apprehension of God (however implicit), we should have no reliable principle to guide us in recognizing a divine revelation in a particular event in history; there would be nothing to justify us in stating that the God of the Bible was, beyond all doubt, our God.

Knowledge of God by faith, therefore, implies two possibilities; one is opened to us by revelation and grace, the other is immanent in reason. This does not mean, however, that the two possibilities are juxtaposed on the same plane, or that the second possibility can make good a deficiency in the first. For one is conditional on an *event*, and the other is *a priori*. The former conditions faith as an *event;* the latter conditions it as regards *meaning*.[27] To say that faith derives from the autonomous reason of the subject is not to admit, however, that it is independent of divine action. Man's natural power of

[27]These formulae, which we have already used in our work on *Karl Barth* (III, 101, 104), have caused some perplexity to our friend Fr L. Malevez. It seemed to him that our thought, if it did not go farther than that, would certainly not arrive at "the notion of a faith ever growing richer in meaning". (*La foi comme événement et comme signification*, in the *Nouvelle Revue Théologique*, April 1959, 385–86.) But to say that natural knowledge of God conditions faith as regards meaning does not at all imply that natural knowledge of God comprises the entire content of faith. We had been careful to make this clear on the following page of our work quoted above (III, 104) in these words: "Neither knowledge of the incarnation nor knowledge of the Trinity is expressly included in the *a priori* of natural knowledge of God". With Fr Malevez and all other theologians we hold (III, 386) that the light of faith brings new meanings with it that cannot be perceived without it.

knowing God comes from the fact that God creates man to his own image. The exercise of this power immediately indicates that God himself has acted upon our spiritual being. We should then say with Barth—whose view here coincides with the view commonly held by the Fathers of the Church—that we can only know God through God; but we must immediately add the essential reminder that it is *we* who can know him.

If it is true that the Christian faith necessarily implies a pre-existing apprehension of God on the part of the subject, the role of what is—not too happily—called "natural theology" is to make explicit this intuitive notion of the divine. This will consist primarily in demonstrating the proof of God's existence. Barth was right, of course, in saying that God has no need of proofs. But we may have need of them. God is his own witness in revelation, but it is we who have to recognize him in it. The function of proof is to reveal the rational structure of such recognition. It gives conceptual form to the assurance we have in our heart of hearts that our belief in God is not arbitrary, and that our Christian thought, submissive and obedient though it be, is really and truly thought. It makes explicit that natural knowledge of God which constitutes the *a priori* condition of knowledge of God by faith.

2. Let us now ask ourselves whether this natural knowledge which is active implicitly in the bosom of the Christian and biblical faith, is not active in some way also, outside it. The New Testament plainly invites us to believe that it is. The first chapter of the Epistle to the Romans and the seventeenth chapter of the Acts of the Apostles are especially clear on this point. The pagans were aware of God, St Paul tells the Romans (1:21). It seems difficult to maintain, as Barth does, that the pagans' knowledge of God was an "imputed" knowledge, belonging "objectively" to their existence in Christ, but entirely absent from their consciousness. Surely the only kind

of knowledge possible is conscious knowledge? How could Paul say that pagan minds were "darkened" (1:21), if no light had ever reached them? How could he reproach them with having "suppressed the truth" (1:18), if they had always been ignorant of the truth? And how could he have declared them to be "without excuse" for failing to recognize the Creator (1:20), if he thought they never had an inkling that there was a Creator? Ignorance is culpable only when it suspects where the truth lies but fails to pursue it. Paul's words here tell us that idolatry itself implies a certain knowledge of God, obscured, it is true, by culpable ignorance.

The speech in the Areopagus attributed to Paul in the Acts of the Apostles (17:22-29) is couched in somewhat different terms. Instead of referring to knowledge darkened by ignorance as a fact, he mentions a natural knowledge of God as a radical possibility; he even suggests that the Athenians' knowledge of God was in some respects, not far removed from the truth. Because God created the world, he tells them, their destiny is to "seek God in the hope that they might feel after him and find him . . . he is not far from each one of us, for 'In him we live and move and have our being'; as even some of your poets have said, 'For we are indeed his offspring'" (17:27-28). There is no question here (though Barth thinks otherwise), of announcing a truth to the pagans, for the first time, through the apostolic message; the pagans know it already. The possibility of knowing God is open to all humanity, and the pagans, in spite of their errors, have entertained, and at times, given expression to ideas about the true God. Paul means to take his stand on this preliminary knowledge, to start from it, to put it in the correct perspective, and so to prepare their minds and hearts to receive the Christian message. The wisdom of the Stoics gives him a point of contact for his preaching.

We cannot, therefore, adopt Barth's thesis, which would prohibit a Christian from admitting that a natural knowledge of God was both possible and legitimate. We agree with Bultmann that there is in every man, Christian or not, a knowledge of God and that without it he could not recognize the gospel message as the Word of God. Shall we say, then, with the same theologian, that natural knowledge is not knowledge of God himself, but simply the consciousness man has of his own limitations? We may be sure that, on philosophical and scriptural grounds, such a statement would be bound to provoke a rather abstruse discussion—and this is not the place for it.

Instead, we will ask ourselves this question: Can we glean anything acceptable from the arguments of Barth and Bultmann against "natural theology" as it is often presented by the Catholic side? The courtesy that dialogue always demands, our sincere desire to ascertain and understand the views of the other parties, and our consciousness that there are certain difficulties to be surmounted, all these invite us to consider carefully what they have to say. Many Catholic treatises or manuals of "natural theology" are not only weak on the philosophical side but are apparently oblivious of the teaching of the Bible and of Christian tradition on the relation between natural knowledge of God and knowledge of God by faith. The criticisms offered by the Protestant theologians, exaggerated though they are, ought to direct our attention to these deficiencies. They ought to persuade us to take a more careful look at the New Testament, and to note the historical and dialectical nature of the knowledge of God.

If St Paul states that the pagans are aware of the true God, he also states that they have failed to acknowledge him and that the only way they can do this is to believe in Christ.[28] He does

[28]See our Karl Barth, III, 119–122.

not advise them to work out a correct natural theology. He asks them to be converted to the Christian faith; only by this can they get to know the true God.

In the apostle's eyes, the pagan consciousness—considered as a historical phenomenon—is idolatrous; every description of this phenomenon is bound to reveal ignorance of the true God. It is only after giving some thought to the matter that it dawns upon him that the idolater has a knowledge of God. Observing that the pagans deify creatures, he wonders how so culpable a custom could ever have come about. Then it occurs to him that it can be explained by the presence in man of an original, inborn idea of God. The pagans would surely never have thought of deifying creatures—and could never have been blamed for doing so—if they had not some innate notion of the divine, some knowledge of God. But, as it happened, that original knowledge had become blurred and perverted in their consciousness and its true content remained implicit and imprisoned; only reflection could bring it to light.

And so, Paul has recourse to the current Stoic philosophy. We can see this in the Epistle to the Romans, and even better in his speech in the Areopagus (*Acts* 17). But if he borrows elements from Stoic thought, he certainly transfigures them. He knows of no way to express the exact meaning of this "original idea of God" except that conforming to biblical and Christian doctrine. For him, indeed, faith is the only true realization of the idea of God.

Every attempt to develop a "natural theology" that would accord with St Paul's teaching, must, in our opinion, be undertaken with the following considerations constantly in mind:

(*a*) "Natural theology" and, in particular, proof of the existence of God, which is the essential part of it, should be directed towards bringing out this "original idea of God" which is implied in all Christian belief (and in every religious attitude), making it conscious of itself, making it, so to speak, explain its own rational structure.

(*b*) Although a Christian's faith can be rational without involving any such methodical operation, it is, nevertheless, necessary that such an exercise shall be capable of being performed. It is, in fact, by means of what we have called the original idea of God that we know the God of the Bible to be our God. This original idea of God must be capable of being expounded in a reasoned treatise, in language intelligible to men of every faith or none; it will be a treatise, therefore, of a general philosophical character.

(*c*) Such a treatise, however, will not look right to Christian eyes if it does not correspond to the intelligible structure of the faith. It must, accordingly, keep in step with the content of the faith even up to the frontiers of theology. Although independent of the faith in theory, it should, in some way, present the faith as it was understood by the Fathers of the Church and the great theologians of the Middle Ages. Little note seems to have been taken of the fact that none of these theologians appears to have thought of developing natural theology as a separate study. St Thomas himself, who allows it more autonomy than most, includes it in theology proper, not only in the *Summa contra Gentiles* but also in the *Summa theologica*.[29] We do not say it is wrong to treat natural theology separately, but it would be well to remember that, by so treating it, we get the rational *intrastructure*, and not, strictly speaking, the infrastructure, of Christian theology. As for the speculative theologian, he will have to take up this task anew and give it a permanent place in his own curriculum.

[29]See Etienne Gilson, *Le Thomisme*, 5th edn. 1948, Introduction.

VI

BULTMANN ON THE PROBLEM OF
DEMYTHOLOGIZATION

Rudolf Bultmann first became known through his *History of the Synoptic Tradition*, which appeared in 1921 and made him one of the creators of the method of form-criticism (*Formgeschichtliche Methode*). But immediately afterwards he again achieved publicity, at least in Germany, with a considerable number of articles of a purely theological nature. Like Barth, he had turned away from the liberal theology propounded by Wilhelm Hermann, and also like Barth and under Barth's influence, he was now drawn towards what came to be called "dialectical theology". For several years he was looked upon as one of the group that went under that label. But the community of thought among its members was, in fact, rent by rifts that quickly deepened and soon brought about the disintegration of the group. In 1928, Bultmann took up the anthropology of Heidegger, and began to use it in his interpretation of Scripture. For this Barth could never wholly forgive him. None the less, and in spite of the rupture of their former relations, they still have something in common. Both reject liberal theology and Protestant orthodoxy. Both believe the Bible to be the Word of God, but both also view the Word of God as an act, as an event, and not as a transmitted doctrine or an established institution.

It is important to bear in mind that, behind all Bultmann's exegetical work, there is a theological motive. His interpretation of the New Testament oversteps the bounds of strictly scientific exegesis. Although in studying the texts he employs the historical-comparative method and maintains a meticulous regard for critical rigour, Bultmann does not treat them as simple primary sources that allow the historian to reconstruct a picture of primitive Christianity considered as a phenomenon of an age long past. He holds that they have a message (*kerygma*) for our age, a message that invites our faith. Any historical reconstruction, he insists, must serve this interpretation. His major works, the "Commentary on John's Gospel" and especially, the "Theology of the New Testament" are theological, as well as historical, works. Bultmann is concerned to interpret the New Testament message in such a way that it is clearly seen to be addressed to ourselves, to our own age, and to invite us to accept it.

Now, the New Testament, he holds, is couched in terms and forms characteristic of mythology and unacceptable to our age. This mythological veil partly hides the reality which its message is meant to convey. In order that the preaching of the New Testament may strike home to us, it must be "demythologized", and the way to demythologize it is to give it an existential interpretation.

Bultmann's major works are devoted to this task. He thought it well, however, to define his programme systematically in a separate article entitled "The New Testament and Mythology

—The Problem of the Demythologization of the New Testament Message".[1] This article, some thirty-five pages long, published in 1941, provoked numerous and interminable discussions, in Germany and elsewhere, among Catholics as well as Protestants, among exegetes, theologians and philosophers. It placed its author in the forefront of contemporary theology and brought him fame from far beyond specialist circles.

It would be unfair to take Bultmann's heremeneutics as tied down to the contents of the article just mentioned, which was only a schematic and incomplete outline. We have to take account of the way in which he subsequently elaborated it and of the way he carried it out in his major works. However, since that article inaugurated his programme and the discussions that continue to rage round it, it might be as well if we were to take a look at its essential features.

1. *Programme for Demythologizing*

The New Testament, says Bultmann, presents a mythical picture of the world (*Weltbild*). It is a world of three storeys. The top storey is the abode of God and the angels; the bottom storey is hell, the place of torment; and the middle storey is the earth on which we live. But the earth is not only the scene of natural events and the works of man; miracles are not infrequent, and man himself, and indeed the whole of history, are subject to the action of supernatural powers, those of God and his angels, and those of Satan and his demons. The present aeon is nearing its end. The end will be marked by the coming

---

[1] *Neues Testament und Mythologie. Das Problem der Entmythologisierung der neutestamentlichen Verkündigung.* Text reproduced in *Kerygma und Mythos*, I (a collection published by H. W. Bartsch, Hamburg 1951). References to this text will be referred to in the notes below by the symbols KM. I, followed by the page number.

of the divine judge, the resurrection of the dead, and the judgement. The essence of the New Testament message, that is to say, the event of salvation (*Heilsgeschehen*), conforms to this mythical picture of the world. The New Testament is couched in mythical language. The last days have now arrived, and God has sent his Son into the world. This Son, a divine, pre-existing being, appears on earth as a man. His death on the cross atones for the sins of men. His resurrection is the beginning of a cosmic catastrophe that annihilates death, which was introduced into the world by Adam. The risen Son of God has been exalted and sits in heaven at the right hand of God. Soon he will return on the clouds of heaven, to complete the work of salvation. The believer, united to him by baptism and communion, is assured that, provided he does not prove himself unworthy, he, too, shall rise from the dead to everlasting blessedness; the Spirit who confers divine sonship on him, has guaranteed that it shall be so.[2]

All this, says Bultmann, is the language of mythology: the supernatural, the divine, is presented as natural and human.[3] Now such language is not acceptable today, because modern thought, formed by science, can no longer admit this mythical image of the world. What sense is there in declaring that Christ "descended into hell" or "ascended into heaven", when we have ceased to believe in a three-storeyed world? Knowledge of the laws of nature makes belief in spirits, demons and miracles obsolete. But it is not only natural science that causes us to criticize; a far more radical cause is modern man's idea of himself (*Selbstverständnis*). Man now regards himself as an autonomous being; his feelings, thought, and will he attributes to himself. He does not imagine, as the New Testament does, that strange powers have taken possession of

[2]KM I, 15–16.
[3]KM , 22, note 2.

his inner being, of his mind and of his heart. What the New Testament says about the action of the Spirit (*pneuma*) and of the sacraments is incomprehensible to him. Unable to understand how his sin could be expiated by the death of an innocent man, he can see no meaning in the doctrine of vicarious satisfaction[4] by the death of Christ. No more does he see how he could draw from the sacraments a vital power liberated by the resurrection of Jesus. A miraculous event in nature, such as the restoration of a dead man to life, besides being incredible, could not, in any event, be a divine action that would change the whole nature of human life. Evangelism today cannot ask the believer to accept this mythology. And so, the question arises whether the New Testament message conveys a truth independent of the mythology. If it does it will be the business of theology to "demythologize" the preaching of the gospel.[5]

It is not a question here of purely and simply *eliminating* mythology; that would risk eliminating the message itself, as was the case in liberal theology. The question is to *interpret* the message critically. The very nature of myth and of certain aspects of the New Testament, invites us to extract the existential sense of the objectifying images in the text, that is to say, the concept of human existence they are meant to convey. This is what Bultmann calls existential interpretation. Modern man will certainly not go to the New Testament for scientific anthropology; he will go to it for fresh knowledge of himself, knowledge that will confront him with a decision.[6]

Once stripped of its mythical disguise (belief in the action of external powers, Jewish apocalyptic mannerisms, and gnostic ideas), the New Testament concept of human existence stands

[4]The doctrine according to which Christ, *representing* mankind, makes satisfaction for the sins of mankind.
[5]KM I, 15–21.
[6]KM I, 21–27.

out as the opposition of the unauthentic life, the life of sin, to
the authentic life, the life of faith, and the passage from the
one to the other. The former consists in wanting to live wholly
on visible things, on what is, or can be, placed at one's disposal;
the latter consists in living on the invisible, which is not at
man's disposal. To believe is to turn oneself towards the
future, to abandon oneself completely to God, and to view
the world in a spirit of detachment (*Entweltlichung*), not in an
ascetic sense, but in the sense of distance. The world must be
used as though one did not use it (*Cor.* 7:29–31). To exist thus
is to exist eschatologically, to be a "new creature".[7]

Such existence has become possible only through the advent
—the *event*—of Christ (*Christusgeschehen*), through God's
action in revealing his love to man.[8] But this event must be
extricated, so to speak, from the objectifying images in the
New Testament, which present it in the manner of a myth.
This mythical presentation was used expressly to show the
universal significance (*Bedeutsamkeit*) of the story of Jesus and
all that Jesus stood for—in other words, their importance as
the symbol and the *event* of salvation.[9] Belief in the cross of
Christ does not consist in the idle contemplation of a mythical
prodigy performed by God for our benefit outside us and our
world. Faith in Christ means taking up Christ's cross and letting
ourselves be crucified with him. The cross as the symbol and
the fact of our salvation is not just an event in the past, an
event to be commemorated; it is an eschatological event that
is in, and yet beyond, time. When its full significance is grasped
by faith, the cross becomes the constant daily companion of
the believer.[10] The resurrection, similarly, can never be con-

---

[7] KM I, 27–31.
[8] KM I, 31–40.
[9] KM I, 40–41.
[10] KM I, 41–43.

ceived as the return of Jesus to the life of this world. It is an action of God, inaccessible to historical research, a pure object of faith. It is an eschatological fact in which the Christian participates in his daily life. The message of the resurrection simply shows the significance of the cross, and faith in this message is nothing but faith in the cross as an event of salvation. The paschal faith of the first disciples constitutes the Easter event in so far as it is accessible to the historian. But otherwise, as in the case of our own faith, it, too, belongs to the eschatological event that constitutes the object of faith. The same must be said of the preaching that derives from it and of the Church which perpetuates that preaching.[11] And so, the eschatological action of God is not a supernatural miracle but a historical (*geschictlich*) event in space and time. It is the human destiny of Jesus, whose meaning is preached by men within that historical phenomenon which is the Church. To see in all this an eschatological event is evidently a paradox, a "scandal", that can only be surmounted by faith. But for that very reason, the transcendence (*Jenseitigkeit*) of God is not transformed into immanence (*zum Diesseits*) as in the myth. What is attested is the paradox of the presence of the transcendent God in history—"the Word was made flesh".[12]

After reading the above rapid summary of Bultmann's 1941 article on the demythologization of the New Testament,[13] we can easily understand the stir it caused among the various Protestant communions. It is obvious that the "demy-

[11]KM I, 44-48.

[12]KM I, 48.

[13]On Karl Barth's reaction to Bultmann's article see, in addition to the work mentioned above, our article entitled *La position d'une théologie réformée en face de l'interprétation existentiale* in the symposium *Il problema della demitizzazione* published by E. Castelli, Rome 1961, 147-156.

thologized" gospel message is a very poor thing indeed. In particular the person and the work of Jesus Christ seem to have lost the place they traditionally occupied in Christian teaching. One is tempted to say: "They have taken away my Lord and I do not know where they have laid him."

But, on the other hand, Bultmann's argument is subtle and well supported; and the author has since shown no lack of resource in replying to objectors. His replies, it is true, leave essential difficulties still unsolved. But, reading them, one realizes how hard it is to pinpoint precisely what is wrong with them. The reason is that Bultmann has put his finger on a real problem and has based his argument on principles that cannot be rejected out of hand. It is not enough, then, to retort with massive protests and ready-made solutions. We must re-think the problem and also re-think the principles involved in solving it. That is no easy task. But the Catholic theologian is undoubtedly better equipped to tackle it than his Protestant counterpart.

Let us approach it first in its most general aspect. Is there any valid reason why the New Testament should be "demythologized"? And must we really give it an existential interpretation? We propose to deal with each of these questions separately.

2. Demythologization

We shall have no room here to discuss side-issues, which, though interesting in themselves, would distract attention from the essential problem.

Several Protestant theologians have objected to Bultmann's thesis on the ground that there is no good reason for demythologizing the New Testament; the language of faith, they say, like the language of religion generally, is necessarily mythological; myth is the very mouthpiece of religion.

Bultmann has replied to this by pointing out, very justly, that they themselves find it necessary to treat the language of the New Testament as symbolic and to interpret it, and that, by doing so, they are doing what he does.

Other critics have accused him of having an inexact, or too strict, or too formal, conception of what myth is. He replies that he has adopted the notion of myth that is in common use among religious historians. We may remark here that, in fact, Bultmann adopted the notion of myth that was current throughout the eighteenth and nineteenth centuries; it implied the opposite of science and put the accent on the fictitious and illusory character of myth. Bultmann did not appear to pay sufficient attention to the fact that, for the past forty years or so, the science of comparative religion has ceased to regard myths as pseudo-scientific explanations of the world and has stressed their meaning and value in human existence. But that is not the important question. Bultmann replies to his critics by saying that he has no wish to impose his notion of myth on anybody; he had adopted it because it seemed a convenient means of conveying what he meant. The real problem, however, lies in what he meant by the word myth.

Myth, to his mind, includes every statement in which the other-worldly appears in worldly guise, in which the divine appears as human and the transcendent as immanent. Every statement, therefore, is a myth that attributes certain phenomena or certain events to supernatural powers, and, in particular, every statement which suggests that God intervenes in the world in the way that a human being would intervene, that is, by an action inserted in a chain of phenomena and therefore capable of being instantly perceived. Such a statement, says Bultmann, is contrary to scientific thought, which can only conceive nature as an immanent causal determinism governed by laws. Moreover, when such a statement suggests that supernatural powers intervene at the very core of human activity, it runs counter to modern man's consciousness of being responsible for his own actions. What is contrary to scientific thought and opposed to the mental make-up of modern man is, in effect, what Bultmann describes as mythical or mythological.

Bultmann takes the view that the New Testament represents God's action in Jesus Christ and in the faithful in such a way that the whole idea of it finds no response in modern minds formed in a scientific atmosphere. And, having read his impressive array of examples from the New Testament, we may well agree that they sound rather odd to our present age. But he goes on to say that we ought not to be put off by these representative examples of what he calls myth; under the veil of myth, they are meant to bring home to us the relationship of our human existence to God. Indeed, he adds, the New Testament even invites us to go beyond the letter of the myth. In fact, it contains passages that have nothing mythological about them and speak to us in plain language; in these we see the New Testament itself initiating the process of demythologization. And Bultmann goes on to show us how, by proceeding on these lines, we can extract the real meaning of the New Testament and leave the mythological deposit behind.

He accordingly proposes two successive courses of New Testament readings. The first consists entirely of mythological matter; the second reveals the authentic meaning of human existence, the authentic gospel message. While the second course of readings interests the philosopher and edifies the believer, the first has a certain Voltairean, quasi-scientific attraction; it shocks the believer but seems rather naive to the philosopher who is well aware that the value of science is a relative one. On further examination we find, however, that the first readings owe their impact to their having been selected and grouped in an *ad hoc*, artificial manner. If it is true, as Bultmann says, that the New Testament itself invites us to demythologize its "mythological" message, it is because that message, considered *in toto* is not mythological. The weighty argument for demythologization turns out to be quite artificial. The most "shocking" part of Bultmann's programme is a purely artificial product.

The language of the New Testament, certainly, borrows largely from Jewish apocalyptic writings and from Hellenistic gnosis, and the expressions it takes over from them naturally have a mythological flavour. But the New Testament incorporates them in a context that demythologizes them. There, in fact, they no longer hint at a mythical process but serve to characterize the work of salvation accomplished in the historical person of Jesus and in the faith of the Church. This reference to the historical event gives the borrowed expressions a new meaning.

When all this is said, it remains true that the language of the New Testament, in so far as it has made such borrowings, does not speak to our generation as it spoke to those who first heard it; its message is no longer a *direct* one. We cannot make it our own unless we interpret it. On this point Bultmann is right, and we are quite willing to acknowledge, with him, that this shows up the poverty of our theology. If the New Testament, considered as a whole, does not require demythologization, perhaps an appreciable number of our theological works and books of devotion do. By repeating the gospel message without interpreting it, they often speak a language foreign to our generation, a language that can frequently seem absurd as well.

Yes, the interpretation of Scripture is an essential duty of contemporary theology. But must this mean existential interpretation, as advocated by Bultmann?

3. *Existential interpretation*

Let us first be quite clear as to what this means. Existential interpretation is interpretation that is concerned with, and guided by, the question of human existence, and its purpose is to bring out what the New Testament says of human existence considered in its relation to God. It is based on the following principle, which Bultmann regards as fundamental. God's action is not a worldly phenomenon capable of objective definition; it cannot be perceived independently of the fact that it concerns me existentially, that is, one cannot speak of it without, at the same time, speaking of me whom it concerns. To speak of God and of his action is to speak, at the same time, of my existence. And so, I can only understand what the New Testament says about God and his action, by understanding what it simultaneously says about my existence.

Now, what does the New Testament say about my existence? It asks me to believe that God forgives me, that I am a sinner made just. Faith in this is not simply a theoretical consent to a theoretical proposition. It is the decision whereby I detach myself from my unauthentic life which is preoccupied with the things the world places at my disposal, in order to embark upon a new kind of life in which I attach myself to something that is not mine to dispose of. In so far as it is a new life detached from the world, faith is eschatological existence.

The New Testament, therefore, when it tells me of God's action, offers me a comprehension of myself that is bound up with an existential decision. The existential interpretation is that which brings out this self-comprehension.

Now, says Bultmann, in order that I may understand what the New Testament tells me about God and myself, I must be conscious of a "lived", and already received, experience of what it tells me; I must have a precomprehension, a preliminary knowledge, of what it speaks about. I must know, for instance, what life and death mean, and what is meant by authentic existence. I must be alive to the question of God. In order to believe it is not absolutely necessary for this precomprehension to be explicit. But this is indispensable for anyone who would set out to give a methodical interpretation of the New Testament and of the Church's official preaching. Existential interpretation, which is work for the exegete-theologian, presupposes, therefore, existential analysis of the human being, an analysis which is the work of the philosopher. The exegete will not require this analysis to tell him what Christian existence ought, in fact, to be; he will only want to know what are the general and formal structures of man's being, considered as existence.

Bultmann borrowed this existential analysis from Heidegger —to be more specific, from the latter's *Sein und Zeit*. There he found an elaboration of what Kierkegaard had already revealed to him—the idea of the historicity of the human being. Man is a temporal being who fulfils himself through decisions in which he chooses himself as his own possibility. Bultmann wants to express the Christian message in terms of the historicity of the human being. That is what he means by existential interpretation.

The result of all this could be to reduce the Christian message to a philosophy. Certain disciples of Bultmann have deliberately set out to do so. But Bultmann himself has always refused to go so far, because, he says, even if philosophy were sufficient to show man his true nature, it would require more than philosophy to make him fulfil it. Man is a sinner. Only the action by which God reveals his love can move man to choose an authentic existence. And this action is revealed to him in the message of the cross and of the resurrection.

What can a Catholic think of existential interpretation as conceived by Bultmann? To my mind, he should accept its basic principles but dispute the methods by which they are applied.

Take the second principle, that which affirms the necessity for a precomprehension. On this point the Catholic theologians agree more fully with Bultmann than do many of their Protestant counterparts. I have already mentioned, in my first chapter—on the nature of apologetics—that the Christian message would have no meaning for us if it did not give us the reply to the question posed by our existence; it can only be understood by the person who puts that question to himself, at least implicitly. We must now add that, in order to work out, step by step, what the message implies, we should have to elucidate, step by step, what the question itself implies. In other words, we cannot dispense with the aid of a philosophy if we want to think out a theology.

It remains to be seen whether the particular philosophy that Bultmann makes use of, is, today at least, the best fitted for the purpose. Although inspired by Heidegger and Kierkegaard, it uses only certain elements of their thought. Anyone familiar with the great classical philosophers must certainly find it jejune. It is incapable of adequately defining man's relation to the world or to history, or his relation to God. It runs the great risk, therefore, of watering down the Christian message. Of all recent philosophical systems, that of Maurice Blondel, rightly interpreted, would be much better adapted to our purpose.

So much for the second of Bultmann's principles of existial interpretation. Let us now go back to the first, which states that one cannot speak of God and his action, without, at the same time, speaking of human existence. But surely the Bible always proceeds in this way? It never tells us of God without telling us what he does for us and within us; and it points out that this revealing and saving action of his is apprehended by us only in so far as it is brought home to us personally and we open our hearts to it. To recognize God's action and to accept a new comprehension of oneself that is also a new life, are one and the same thing. On this point we agree with Bultmann.

We could then go on to examine his idea of justification by faith and eschatological existence in faith. But that would take us too far off our course. What is of immediate interest to us here is the relation between faith and Christ, between eschatological existence and the eschatological event.

In this connection, Bultmann uses a very striking phrase: "The eschatological event that is Christ takes place uniquely *in concreto*, here and now, when the Word is preached, whether to the faithful or to unbelievers".[14] The question is to know whether the being and the role that the New Testament attributes to the historical person of Jesus Christ, are volatilized in the process. Let us now examine this idea of the event of Christ.

4. *The Event of Christ*

Bultmann, as we have seen, holds that the event of Christ is presented in the New Testament in the form and style of a myth. Jesus Christ, Son of God, a pre-existing divine being, who appears on earth as a man, who attests his divinity by miracles, whose death makes full atonement for man's sins, and whose bodily resurrection destroys the powers of death— all this is a mythical theme told in the language of myth. But this Jesus Christ is, at the same time, presented as a man, Jesus of Nazareth; and the destiny of that person is a human destiny that ends on a cross. This mixture of myth and history, says Bultmann, suggests that the purpose of the mythological

---

[14]*Zum Problem der Entmythologisierung* in *Kerygma und Mythos*, II, 206.

language is simply to stress the meaning and import of the historical figure of Jesus and of his life on earth, their symbolic meaning and their significance as the saving event in man's salvation. Once the true meaning of the gospel message is extracted from the content of the myth, what is left serves no further purpose. Bultmann justifies this interpretation theologically by appealing to a celebrated proposition of Melanchton, which is, indeed, a summary of the early thought of Luther: "We know Christ, not by considering his natures and the intricacies of the incarnation, but by knowing the blessings he has brought us."

Let us take a closer look at Bultmann's procedure. In an article devoted to the Christological Confession of the World Council of Churches,[15] he passes in review the various divine titles which the New Testament gives to Jesus—Messiah, Son of man, Lord, Son of God, God. Then he explains that the basic idea behind these titles is not to give us information about the nature of Jesus, not to objectify his being-in-itself, but rather to express what Jesus signifies for man, for faith. They mean that, in what Jesus says, in what he is, God speaks to us, God acts upon us, God acts for us. They show how the advent of Jesus has placed man in a new situation, has called on him to decide for or against God; how believers have been snatched from the world and made new creatures. The formula "Christ is God" is, therefore, incorrect if the word God is taken to be an objectifiable power in the Arian, Nicean, orthodox, or liberal sense. It is correct if God is understood as the event that is the outcome of God's action.

In the famous article "The New Testament and Mythology" which we summarized early in this chapter, Bultmann, as we have seen, gives a similar explanation of the message of the

[15]Reprinted in *Glauben und Verstehen*, II, 246–61.

cross and of the resurrection. The idea of a sacrifice that would atone for the sins of mankind is a mythological one and, says Bultmann, we of a more scientifically-oriented age, cannot accept it. But its role is essentially to express the import of the historical event of the cross. It tells us that this historical event is a judgement passed on the world, that it places us in a new situation. To believe in the cross of Christ is not to turn our thoughts back to an event in the past; it is to let oneself be crucified with Christ. The event that occurred in the past keeps on recurring in the present (*Gegenwart*); it recurs in the preaching of the Word, in the sacraments and in the everyday life of the Christian. And because of that it has an eschatological character.

How do we discover that the historical event of the cross signifies or implies all this? Bultmann insists that we cannot discover it solely by considering the historic life of Jesus. We can grasp it only through faith in the preaching of the Word, which always presents Christ as crucified *and* risen from the dead. To speak of Christ's resurrection is simply to proclaim the message of the cross. To believe in the resurrection is not to believe in the incredible miracle of the restoration of a dead man to life, it is to believe that the cross of Christ places us in a new situation. And how are we to perceive that and believe in it? Solely by the fact that the cross is preached *with* the resurrection. We encounter Christ crucified and risen in the *preaching* of the Word, and nowhere else. It would be wrong to seek to verify and justify the content of the preaching by a study of its historical origin. We can only believe it, or refuse our belief.

How will a Catholic theologian react to this interpretation? Leaving aside the problem of the resurrection—which is too complex to be disposed of in a line or two—let us concentrate on the question of the divine titles given to Jesus, and on the message of the cross. For the reasons already mentioned we will not say that the language of the New Testament in this context is mythological. We will agree, however, that it is bound up with ways of thinking and expressing thought in language, which our generation cannot immediately understand. We cannot take the scriptural language literally; we have to interpret it. We cannot accept what it seems to say without explaining what it says.

On the other hand, we must not forget that, where God and his action are concerned, all human language, ancient and modern, is necessarily *analogical*. The statements made in Scripture, and in the preaching that interprets it, do not depict God in himself, or his action in so far as it is his. Such statements depict them in their relation to us; that is, we have certain relations with God and his action, and it is in the form of these relations that God and his action are always depicted. St Thomas puts it in this way: "We do not know who God is, but only what he is not, and what relation everything else has with him".[16] St Thomas makes it clear that this holds good also in the case of revelation. Revelation, he says, does not give us knowledge of what God is; it gives us knowledge of him in so far as it tells us of his works.[17] There is a curious resemblance between this statement and one that recurs like a *leitmotiv* throughout Bultmann's work: we cannot tell what God is in himself; we can only tell of what he does in us and for us.[18] Yes, the Thomist doctrine of analogy would allow us to take over all that is best in Bultmann's programme, although we might not use it in the way he does. It must, indeed, be admitted that theologians, even Catholic ones—and Thomists at that—

---

[16]*Contra Gentiles*, I, 30, end. An exposition of the Thomist doctrine of analogy will be found in our work *Karl Barth*, III, 198–204.

[17]*S. theol.*, Ia, q. 12, a. 13, ad 1.

[18]KM II, 185.

too often forget this doctrine. They comment on Scripture without recalling that the *res significata* can be reached only through the negation of the *modus significandi*. They speak of divine things as if these were human things. Consequently, their commentaries often have a mythological ring, and provoke the sort of criticism that Bultmann levels quite unreasonably at the New Testament.

Let us start from the principle that we only know God and his action from his work and from the relation everything else has with him. It now remains to be seen whether the work that God accomplishes in Jesus Christ consists solely in transforming *our existence* by faith in the Word as preached by the Church, in the new relation *we* thereby contract with God. But would it not consist initially of a unique relation of the *man Jesus* with God, a relation that would afterwards become, in our Christian faith, the mediating agent of our new relation with God? God acts in us when the preaching of the Word enlivens our faith in Christ; and his saving action only touches us so long as we have faith. But, it is also certain, from the New Testament, that God first acted in Jesus of Nazareth, establishing Jesus in a unique relation with him, in order thereby to induct ourselves into a new relation with him.

Why should this action of God in Jesus be more mythical than the action of God in us? True, the divine action in us concerns and impinges upon our own existence, and so it can be spoken of in plain, non-mythological language. But why should there not be an action of God in Jesus that would concern and impinge upon the existence of Jesus, making his existence the ex-sistence of God himself in the world? In short, could not one give an existential interpretation from the christology of the New Testament that would maintain the truth of the traditional dogma?

Pertinent suggestions in this regard are to be found in an

essay by Fr Karl Rahner on "Current Problems in Christ-ology".[19] The author does not set out to discuss Bultmann but to show that the dogmatic definition of the Council of Chalcedon declaring that Christ is true God and true man, does not exhaust all that the Bible tells us about Christ. He sets out, therefore, to complete the "ontic" christology emanating from Chalcedon by an existential christology, drawn directly from the New Testament. A rigorous interpretation of the words of Jesus on his spiritual relationship to God the Father would lead, he says, to "the assertion of a conscious relationship of the man Jesus with respect to God, asserting it in such a way that the assertion of the distinctively unique character of this relationship is *eo ipso* an implicit or explicit assertion of the hypostatic union".[20] Anybody who would say, for example: "Jesus is the man whose life is one of absolutely unique self-surrender to God" could very well have expressed the essential being of Christ in all its profundity. That is, provided he has understood that this self-abandonment presupposes and implies an absolute communication of God to the man Jesus, one which makes what is produced by it into the reality of the producer himself.[21]

We have sufficient grounds here for giving the divine titles of Jesus in the New Testament a non-mythological meaning. They do not tell us straight out that Christ was a God who had assumed human form. They tell us he is a man whose life is one of absolutely unique self-surrender to God. They point to the unique relationship of the man Jesus with God, and to the divine origin of that relationship. They do not refer us, there-fore, to a mythical being, but to a real being, to a historical

[19]*Schriften zur Theologie*, I, Einsiedein 1954; Eng. trans. C. Ernst O.P., *Theological Investigations*, Baltimore-London 1961, I, 173.

[20]*Loc. cit.*, 173.

[21]*Loc. cit.*, 172.

existence. And that existence is the ex-sistence of God himself in history.

We have sufficient grounds, too, for giving a non-mythological meaning to the New Testament account of Christ's death on the cross as a redemptive sacrifice. In fact, Christ's death, freely accepted by him in a spirit of obedience and love, was the act by which Jesus consummated his absolutely unique self-surrender to God. By that death, the tragic destiny of mankind became, in Jesus, and by him for other men, the manifestation and the constructive sign of absolute obedience to God, the act by which man fully acknowledges his own finiteness, his fundamental contingency, and definitively abandons himself to God. This is no place to go fully into the doctrine of the redemption. I have only tried to make the point that it loses whatever mythological savour it may have had as soon as we realize that the redemptive act is an act performed in authentic human liberty, an act freely and consciously undertaken, in order to bring about a new relation between mankind and God.

Why did Bultmann throw overboard part of the New Testament doctrine we have just discussed? Why does he attach so little importance, in his christology, to human existence and to the human destiny of Jesus of Nazareth? Could it be because historical criticism convinced him that we can know practically nothing about Jesus? But we do not need to know much more than Bultmann himself retains, in order to give a historical basis to the findings we have set out above. No, Bultmann's motive in rejecting part of the New Testament tradition seems to lie elsewhere.

In our opinion that motive must be sought in Bultmann's Lutheranism. Two features, indeed, are characteristic of the christology of Luther and Lutheranism. On the one hand, it is less interested in what Christ is in himself than in what he is for us. On the other hand, the Lutheran principle that salvation is the work of God alone inhibits Bultmann from assigning an active role in the redemption to Christ's humanity; God acts under the veil of Christ's humanity, and that is all. Consequently, the only thing that counts is the divine promise of salvation and the faith that cherishes it; the history recounted in the New Testament is, in itself, history and nothing more. Obviously Bultmann has been guided by his Lutheran convictions, and it is these that have led him to attach so little importance to the historical person of Jesus Christ.

Another Lutheran conviction, reinforced by reading Kierkegaard, led Bultmann to look upon revelation as pure paradox, and faith as a decision devoid of any rational ground. He tells us so himself. Radical demythologization (he says) by stripping our faith of every shred of human security, only extends to the domain of knowledge the Lutheran doctrine of justification by faith alone, without the works of the Law.[22]

We ourselves, certainly, have no hesitation in admitting that the presence, or the action, of God in history cannot be verified in the way in which a phenomenon can be verified. That is true also of a miracle. We can only believe in God's revelation; and the ultimate basis of that belief is nothing else than the object of belief itself, the presence, and the action, of God.

But that does not imply, as Bultmann would have it, that the Christian message can produce no credentials to attest its truth, that we have no reason for believing, that our faith is "so to speak, suspended in mid air".[23] God, indeed, acts and reveals himself through the medium of certain creatures, and these are *signs* of his presence; such signs are the humanity of Jesus, his doctrine, life and miracles, and the historical reality

[22]KM II, 207.
[23]KM II, 207.

that is the Church. These signs, of course, can fail to be understood; they can even be objects of scandal. But all who understand what they mean find in them a sure support; revelation is no paradox to the believer, who discerns divine revelation in the signs that manifest it. Faith is not suspended in mid air; it perceives revelation in the visible signs inserted by divine action in the reality of the world around us.

We look in vain through Bultmann's work for any mention of *sign* or of the cognate idea of *mediation*. Bultmann did not omit these through ignorance or by accident. His Lutheran faith convinces him that the world is wholly profane, that there is not one iota of sanctity in it, and that when God's action is manifested there, it is manifested against all seeming. To look for signs of God in such a world would be to display an attitude of disbelief.[24]

We can see, then, how Bultmann's interpretation of the New Testament is largely determined by his Lutheran convictions. True, these are not the only factors involved, and by themselves they would not necessarily lead up to his conclusions. Other elements in his thought play their part. Bultmann has a certain existential philosophy, a rather harsh rationalism, and a peculiar idea of the exegetical method proper to the study of the New Testament; the results of that method contribute much to his conclusions. But even these are exploited and fitted into a Lutheran perspective.

By detaching the sound elements in Bultmann's principles and in the results of his literary and historical criticism from their Lutheran setting, a Catholic theologian would arrive at a somewhat different interpretation of the New Testament, but it would be an interpretation which, thanks to Bultmann, would bring it nearer to our own generation.

[24]KM II, 207-8.

PART THREE

Philosophical Approaches

VII

GABRIEL MARCEL AND THE MYSTERY OF BEING

Gabriel Marcel was born in Paris on 7 December, 1889. His father, a counsellor of State, was for a short time French Minister in Stockholm, and afterwards director, successively, of the *Musée des Beaux-Arts*, the *Bibliothèque Nationale* and the *Musées nationaux*. Thanks to his father, a man of prodigious culture, great care was taken with Gabriel's moral and intellectual formation from childhood up. The care may have been excessive but at least it gave him opportunities for enlarging his experience by travelling abroad, and mixing in political and literary circles at home. It is recorded that at the age of eighteen he carried off a *diplôme d'études supérieures* with a thesis on the metaphysical ideas of Coleridge and their bearing on the philosophy of Schelling. He was only twenty when he obtained his *agrégation* in philosophy, and this gave him entry to the teaching profession. But he taught only intermittently—at Vendôme in 1912, in Paris from 1915 to 1918, at Sens from 1919 to 1922; during the last war he taught in Paris again in 1939-40, and at Montpellier in 1941. His main activities have been divided between literary criticism, the theatre, and philosophical research—three distinct domains connected, so to speak, by the same underground source.[1]

His criticism, scattered throughout a most heterogeneous assortment of reviews and weeklies, is concerned principally with the theatre, but fiction, philosophy, poetry and music are also discussed. His aim always is to bring out the human significance and spiritual value of the work reviewed. His curiosity extends to the literature of other countries as well as his own, and he is particularly at home in the literatures of the English-speaking countries, and of Germany. The Plon series, *Feux croisés*, consisting of translations of foreign masterpieces, is edited by him.

His dramatic work is closely bound up with his philosophical research. "It is in drama and through drama that metaphysical thought grasps and defines itself *in concreto*."[2] Anyone who has ever dropped in at one of the philosophical "at homes" given regularly by Marcel for so many years, must have noticed how his thought used to develop as he analysed the implications of a concrete situation. Drama and philosophical reflection are for him "twin peaks of equal height". At the outset of his spiritual evolution, his drama even outstripped his abstract thought, as if the characters he had created divined before he did the hidden profundities of the play and dragged it out of the idealist atmosphere in which it had been set. His drama is

[1]More detailed biographical information will be found in *Existentialisme chrétien: Gabriel Marcel*, in the series *Présences*, Paris 1947, 203–14 (by Roger Troisfontaines) and 291–319 (by G. Marcel). This work contains, amongst other contributions, an excellent study by Jeanne Delhomme. See also M-.M. Davy, *Un philosophe itinérant*, Paris 1959. The most important work on Marcel's philosophy is that of Roger Troisfontaines, *De l'Existence à l'Être. La philosophie de Gabriel Marcel*, Paris 1953 (2 vols.).

[2]*Position et approches concretes du Mystére ontologique* in *Le Monde cassé*, Paris 1933, 277.

never only the mouthpiece of an ideology. The conflicts he presents *exist*, before they are resolved. They depict man's loneliness, painful misunderstandings, obstacles to the course of true love. Scarcely a gleam of hope lightens some of them. This is all the more surprising in that he exalts the merits of a metaphysic of communion and hope. Perhaps it is explained by the fact that, in his own case, harmony between life and men, happiness, friendship and joy always find expression in a different medium—musical improvization.

Gabriel Marcel is known principally for his philosophical work, whose influence has been profound. Many owe to him their spiritual awakening, or the discovery or recovery of their spiritual bearings. During the years immediately following the last war, the affinity of his thought with the several varieties of existential philosophy then in vogue, brought him a still wider audience. Many young Christians saw in it a counterpoise to the existentialism of Jean-Paul Sartre. Marcel's reputation grew abroad as well as at home. He has given numerous lectures in most of the major countries of the world. His work received its crowning tribute when he was invited to deliver the Gifford Lectures in 1949 and 1950.[3]

Marcel's philosophical work is liable to be disconcerting on first approach. Its form is all its own. The first of his books, which came out in 1927, has the paradoxical title *Journal Métaphysique*. The second, *Être et Avoir* (1935), is a sequel. A few lectures and articles round off his work. The books *Du Refus à l'Invocation* (1940) and *Homo Viator* (1944) are collections of articles and lectures. The texts of his books often look like fragments of a journal; they are undated and grouped under subjects. None of his works makes any attempt to

[3]These lectures delivered at the University of Aberdeen, have been published in two volumes under the title *Le Mystére de l'Être:* I. *Réflexion et Mystere:* II. *Foi et Realité*, Paris 1951. (English trans. by R. Hague, London 1951).

develop a train of thought systematically. In 1944 he admitted this himself. "Today," he said, "I can see more and more clearly the reasons why I have not been able to write that treatise I should have so much liked to write; some of those reasons are sound, others are not, but be that as it may, I have now come to the melancholy conclusion that I shall never write it."[4]

It certainly cannot be said that he has written it so far. Even *Le Mystère de l'Être* (1951), which might be regarded as a summing-up of his thought, is just as amorphous as his other works; it is merely a further collection of lectures and articles.

But the reader should not let himself be put off by this departure from "the rules of the philosophic game". It is regrettable, no doubt, but what can we do but write it off as a display of the reverse side of Marcel's excellent qualities? It is partly explained by the author's own conception of his work. The philosopher is man trying to shed light on man's condition. Now man is located in the world, and the philosopher, therefore, cannot disregard the fact that man *of necessity* occupies a certain situation. "The essence of man is to be in a situation." It is not given to the philosopher to ensconce himself in the heart of being, in a sort of central observatory, and to contemplate from there the world in its totality, above and beyond particular perspectives. How then can he aspire to "cork up the universe" with a collection of logically articulated formulae that would, so to speak, deliver the universe into his hands?

No, the philosopher will distrust all system. He will keep in close and constant touch with the concrete. To philosophize concretely is to philosophize "here and now", "to be receptive to reality", never to take the fact of existence as a matter of

[4]*Homo Viator*, Paris 1944, 5. (English trans. London 1951).

course, but always to be alive to its surprises and its wonders. Marcel looks on philosophical effort as "much more like deep drilling than surface erection".[5] It consists, he says, primarily in exploring certain spiritual situations, first delineating them as exactly as possible, and then reflecting on them in order to present them for our inward scrutiny.[6] It could indeed be said that this is a matter of phenomenological analysis with an ontological orientation.

Gabriel Marcel started on his philosophical journey from idealism. Bradley's ideas attracted him at one period. In the beginning, he came under the spell of post-Kantian philosophy. Schelling, in particular, he found congenial, because his comprehensive philosophizing seemed to point the way to a higher empiricism that would satisfy his own craving for the individual and the concrete. The first part of the *Journal Métaphysique* is characterized by a complicated and paradoxical effort to transcend idealism, and to do so by penetrating to the very heart of idealism itself, and looking there for the concrete.

It was by critically examining objective knowledge, as understood by the various forms of idealism, that Marcel came to develop his own train of thought. His criticism was concentrated on the two frontiers of knowledge: on the one side, sensation and the incarnate nature of man; on the other, faith. It led him to see, away beyond objectivity, the reality of existence, on the one hand, and on the other hand, the reality of *Being*, of the Transcendent; between the two and deriving from both, he perceived the reality of the *thou*.

Meditation on what is incorrectly called the problem of soul and body has a capital importance. I am always tempted to

[5] *Du Refus à l'Invocation*. Paris 1940, 23.

[6] *Ibid.*, 158.

regard my body as an instrument, as a tool. But it requires little thought to make me realize that this falls short of the fact. My body cannot be a tool since it is the indispensable condition for the existence of tools at all. In a certain sense, *I am* my body. Materialism has a right understanding of this, and yet the materialist thesis is false because it confuses *my body for me* with *my body for, and among, others*, the body-subject with the body-object. "To be incarnate is to be visible to oneself as body, as this body, without being able to identify oneself with it and yet without being able to distinguish oneself from it."[7] To borrow the language of Heidegger—which Marcel could not have known at the time, as his first books appeared before the former's *Sein und Zeit*—my body is my manner of being in the world. It is an "immediacy", an irreducible datum—the basis, indeed, of all data—which cannot become an object for me, because I have to rely on it to consider every object. I cannot, however, regard it as unknowable. That would still be to degrade it to the level of an object; besides, my body is the condition of all knowledge. And so, for the Cartesian *cogito*, which "guards the threshold of validity", and for the transcendental *I* of Kant, Marcel substitutes the incarnate being as the condition of access to reality and as "the central landmark of metaphysical reflection".

A similar critical examination of sensation leads him to analogous conclusions. I am tempted to think of sensation as a message sent out by a transmitting-station—the object—and received by my sensory apparatus. But, on going more closely into the matter, I conclude that this is not so, since a message is only possible on the basis of sensation. There again I find myself confronted with an "immediacy", an irreducible datum.

Reflection on sensation and incarnate being, therefore, takes

[7] *Ibid.*, 31.

us out of idealism and brings us to recognize, beyond the objective world and the epistemological subject, a world of presence, of here-and-now-ness, of existence.

In the same way, reflection on faith confronts us with Being. From the moment Marcel began to philosophize, the question of faith forced itself upon him. Brought up in a non-religious environment, he always felt unaccountably distressed by the devitalized atmosphere in which he had to live. But it was not until 1929 that he became converted to Catholicism. Curiously enough, the first pages of the *Journal Métaphysique*, which date from 1914, show that, although he had no thought of conversion then, he was already preoccupied with the reality of God. While, to all appearances, still an unbeliever, he believed in the genuineness of the faith of others and analysed its conditions with such penetration that he never felt any need to revise these views. Some months before formally adhering to the Catholic Church, he defended, against Léon Brunschvicg, the very notion of religious faith, during a memorable session of the *Société française de Philosophie*, devoted to "The Case for Atheism" (24 March 1928).

From the very outset of his philosophical career, also, it seemed to him that *I believe* is not reducible to *I think*. This does not mean that the act of faith cannot be thought; it can be thought—but only from within itself. The subject that believes is not thought in general, but the existent. The *I believe* is linked with the *I exist*. Faith is an affirmation which I am, rather than an affirmation which I utter. It is bound to partake of the nature of sensation, based like it on the immediacy of an irreducible datum.[8] The role of metaphysics is to rediscover this immediacy by reflection, and what lies beyond reflection.

In attempting this, we have to guard against treating God as

[8]*Journal Métaphysique*, Paris 1927, 131 (English trans., London 1952); *Du Refus à l'Invocation*, 219.

an object. "When we speak *of* God, we must bear in mind that it is not of *God* we speak."[9] "God can only be given to me as Absolute Presence in worship; every idea I form of him is only an abstraction, an intellectualization of that presence."[10] Like the adepts of negative theology, Marcel considers that what we call God's attributes are nothing more than the marks by which we distinguish him from the idols with which we are liable to confuse him. In other words, they are the defensive ramparts erected in concentric circles around the central affirmation of which I am so much an integral part that I am no longer able to utter it. I really know God only when, in prayer, I surrender myself to him who is my sole recourse, and invoke him as the absolute *Thou*.[11]

If God is essentially a *Thou* for whom I exist, I can readily conceive that he can *not-be* for my neighbour. Proof of God supposes that one is already convinced he exists. It always refers back to faith and can only confirm what faith has already given us. "If the ontological proof still holds good, it is because it is established in God at the outset."[12]

It is evident that such a train of thought must also involve reflection on the relation of individual beings to one another. Gabriel Marcel, indeed, has always been concerned with the transcendent and the individual in conjunction; with the "exigence of *being*" and with "the obsession of beings acutely conscious of their individuality and also of their being enmeshed in the mysterious relations that bind them together".[13] This second preoccupation of his at first found more direct

[9]*Journal Métaphysique*, 158.

[10]*Être et Avoir*, Paris 1935, 248. (English trans. "Being and Having", London 1949).

[11]*Journal Métaphysique*, 254-5; *Du Refus à l'Invocation*, 53-4, 80.

[12]*Journal Métaphysique*, 255; *Être et Avoir*, 141, 175-6, *Du Refus à l'Invocation*, 231-2.

[13]*Du Refus à l'Invocation*, 192-3.

expression in his dramatic work than in his speculative essays. From 1918 onwards, however, it assumed more and more importance in the latter and led to some decisive results. During the first World War he had been engaged in tracing persons who had been reported missing. Every day moving appeals reached him from distressed parents and relatives. About the same time, too, he took part in some metaphysical experiments. He witnessed the steady emergence in the human person of the *thou* that transcends the *he*. The philosophy of Royce, on which he wrote a monograph, taught him something new about this.[14] "When I speak of someone in the third person, I treat him as unconnected with myself, as a person absent and apart; to be more precise, I define him implicitly as exterior to a dialogue in progress, which may very well be a dialogue with myself."[15] When I engage in conversation with a stranger in a train, he appears to me first as "this person here" whose tastes, life and so on I am gradually getting to know. "But it may well happen that I become more and more conscious I am having a dialogue with myself (which does not mean at all that the other person and I are, or even appear to be, identical)."[16] The other person more and more enters into a unity with me. We actually become *us*, and it is because of this that he is *thou*.

The *thou* that is given to us is a *thou* beyond objectivity; it is given as *presence*. It is to this transobjective reality that love and fidelity are related. This implies an Absolute. The unconditional love of the creature for the creature is like the "pre-natal palpitation" of man's faith in the Absolute Thou.[17]

[14]*La Métaphysique de Royce*, essay published in *la Revue de Métaphysique et de Morale* in 1917–8 and reprinted in book form, Paris 1945.
[15]*Journal Métaphysique*, 137.
[16]*Ibid.*, 146.
[17]*Du Refus à l'Invocation*, 179.

Marcel's thought is here found to converge towards that of Martin Buber, but Buber's thought does not exercise any reciprocal influence. Moreover, it is from love that we derive our hope of immortality, a hope that wells up from the secret springs of the loving heart.

In the course of a discussion at the International Philosophical Congress of 1937, in Paris, Brunschvicg, who thought that hope of immortality was a symptom of selfishness and egoism, remarked to Marcel: "The death of Léon Brunschvicg interests Léon Brunschvicg much less than the death of Gabriel Marcel interests Gabriel Marcel". Marcel's reply (in substance) was: "Let us admit that egoism is behind my preoccupation with my death. But what are we to think of an attitude of complete indifference towards the death of somebody one loves?"[18] To love somebody is to say to him or her, "You, certainly, shall never die".

Whether he is discussing the *existence* in which I am immersed by reason of the fact that I am an incarnate being, or the *thou* which I share with another in personal communication, or the *Being* to whom I adhere by my faith, Marcel's fundamental purpose is always the same. "Perhaps it would be true enough", he writes, "to say that, in all my philosophical work, my chief and constant preoccupation was to discover how the subject in its capacity as subject, is linked with a reality that ceases to be capable of being represented as an object *vis-à-vis* that subject, without ever ceasing on that account to be at the same time necessitated and recognized as reality."[19] The subject cannot contemplate reality as if it were set out before him like a picture, because he is involved in it himself, because he, too, is part of the picture. He is not merely

[18]Quoted by Gaston Fessard in the Introduction to Marcel's play, *La Soif*, Paris 1938, 40.
[19]*Regard en arrière*, in *Existentialisme chrétien*, 318.

confronted with a *problem;* he is participating in a *mystery.* This now famous distinction gives us the key to Gabriel Marcel's philosophy. It was implicit in his work from the very beginning, and it became explicit for him after his conversion to Catholicism. He explained it in 1933 in his *Position et Approches concrètes du Mystère ontologique,* a lecture given at a session of the *Société de Philosophie de Marseille* and subsequently published as an appendix to his play *Le Monde cassé.* It is the most compact and forceful of all his works and has been rightly described as his "Introduction to Metaphysics". It would be well to supplement it by reading the contemporary notes reprinted in his *Être et Avoir.*[20]

"A problem is something that blocks my path. It is entirely in front of me. A mystery, on the other hand, is something in which I am involved; its essence, therefore, is not to be entirely in front of me. It is as if in that particular zone the distinction *in me* and *in front of me* loses its significance."[21] "A mystery is a problem that encroaches on, that overruns, its own data, and thereby transcends itself as a problem in the ordinary sense of the word."[22] It is a meta-problem, beyond the sphere of problems.

Consequently, the union of soul and body, evil, love and liberty are not problems but mysteries. I cannot treat them as objects placed in front of me; I am involved in them; they form an integral part of me. And so there is no problem of being, but a *mystery of being.* Under the dual influence of idealism and Bergsonianism, Marcel long fought shy of the idea of being. But at the same time he felt a craving for an inexhaustible *concrete,* a solid stable absolute, thanks to which life would

[20]In particular, 144–79; Marcel resumes this discussion in *Le Mystère de l'Être,* I, 227–8.
[21]*Être et Avoir,* 145.
[22]*Position . . . 267.*

be something more than "a tale told by an idiot"; in
other words, he felt the deep inward urge of ontological
exigence, of the exigence of being. It seemed more and more
imperative "to put its ontological weight back into human
experience",[23] in an empty world where man, degraded by
technology to a mere system of functions, is left with a life
that can only issue in despair. Thanks to the notion of mystery,
our philosopher recaptures, by his own reflective effort, the
exigence of being. And it turns out to be an affirmation "that
I *am*, rather than an affirmation which I *utter*, which I can put
into words", an affirmation "of which I am the source rather
than the subject".[24] It expresses what I must needs *participate in*,
even without my knowledge. And so, "knowledge is enveloped in being", "knowledge is in some way interior to
being", and, just as there is a mystery of being, there is "a
mystery of cognition".[25]

But this means that Being, although "meta-problematical"
and a mystery, is not unknowable. A special effort of the mind
can rescue it from the constant temptation to degrade it by
objectifying it. This special intellectual effort Marcel calls
"secondary reflection" (*réflexion seconde*); it is a deeper, more
intense re-thinking of one's first thought. Secondary reflection
is for him the tool *par excellence* of metaphysical thought. It is
"reflection raised to the second power (*une réflexion à la
deuxième puissance*) and is based upon an experience of
presence",[26] and is, therefore, a negation of negation, dependent

[23] *Être et Avoir*, 149.
[24] *Position* . . . 266.
[25] *Ibid.*, 267.
[26] *Être et Avoir*, 166. Translator's note: Marcel conceives *presence* as an inward
realization of presence, through love, which transcends all verification, because
it has the immediacy of an irreducible datum. (Cf. his essay tr. by M. Harari
under the title of "On the Ontological Mystery", one of three essays in "The
Philosophy Existence", London 1948.)

on a kind of intuition. But the word "intuition" must be used with reserve. Being cannot be perceived, it can only be evoked. In one sense, I see Being, but in another sense, I do not see it, because I cannot catch myself in the act of seeing it. "This intuition is not, and cannot be, a direct object of thought." But, as it flashes through our minds, it casts its transcendental light upon a whole world of hitherto obscure thoughts.[27] It is an "inhibited intuition" and secondary reflection tends to release it.

There is an intuition of this sort at the root of love, fidelity and hope. Marcel lovingly analyses these attitudes in order to show the ontological exigence that they imply, albeit unwittingly. They are for him the "concrete approaches of the ontological mystery".

But they are approaches that are always being threatened. Just because they are dependent on an inhibited intuition, the reality they discern can always be questioned. The structure of our world is such that infidelity and despair are always possible, and, with them, the refusal, the denial, of being. Death, in particular, is a perpetual invitation to despair and betrayal. "An effective refutation *is bound* to be impossible here: despair is irrefutable. We can only come down firmly on one side or the other, for it is beyond the scope of argument."[28] Recognition of the mystery is a *free* act in the bosom of an *experience*. That is why it has always the import of a *creative attestation*. It is thus that we perceive "the hidden identity of the path that leads to holiness and the way that leads the metaphysician to the affirmation of being".[29] Reflection on holiness is perhaps "the real introduction to ontology".[30]

[27] *Être et Avoir*, 142.
[28] *Ibid.*, 160.
[29] *Ibid.*, 123.
[30] *Position* . . . 296.

Such a philosophy is obviously polarized by the Christian revelation, and has only been able to develop on ground prepared by Christianity. But it does not pretend that the Christian revelation is indispensable to it in the first instance, nor does it claim, strictly speaking, to understand that revelation. It does not confuse divinely revealed mysteries with mysteries that are enveloped in human experience. It does not demand adherence to Christianity, although it can, to a certain extent, prepare for the acceptance of Christianity.[31]

For Marcel recognition of the ontological mystery is the keynote of metaphysics. It distinguishes not only between mystery and problem, but also between *being* and *having* (which, basically, is much the same). It inspires the concrete analyses in *Du Refus à l'Invocation* and *Homo Viator*. It forms the nucleus of that summary of Marcel's thought which is unequivocally entitled *Le Mystère de l'Être*. It is worthy of special note that it runs right through the lectures on *le Mystère familial* and on *le Voeu créateur comme essence de la paternité*, which form part of *Homo Viator*, and bring out clearly the connection between the carnal and the spiritual. The whole of this work shows Marcel's preoccupation with maintaining fidelity to the world, while maintaining hope of salvation. "There is," he writes, "a permanent value in Orphism,"[32] and so he puts forward Rilke as a "witness to the spiritual".[33] These views only make explicit the constant association, in Marcel's thought, between the immediacy of sensation and the immediacy of faith, between the mystery of existence and the mystery of being.[34]

---

[31]*Être et Avoir*, 174–5; *Position* . . . 298–301.

[32]*Homo Viator*, II.

[33]*Ibid.*, 297–358.

[34]Marcel's most recent works, *Les Hommes contre l'Humain*, Paris 1951; *Le Déclin de la Sagesse*, Paris 1954; *L'Homme Problématique*, Paris 1955; are chiefly

Marcel's philosophy has been called "speculative mysticism"; this would be a fair enough description if it did not tend to hide the fact that it has always been nourished on the most everyday experience. It has also been called "mystical empiricism", a legitimate label provided it is borne in mind that, for Marcel's thought, experience is meaningful only when interpreted by creative reflection. Finally, it has been termed "Christian existentialism"; to this Marcel, a short time ago, gave his consent reluctantly, and with reservations.

Unquestionably there is a resemblance between his thought and the various contemporary philosophies of existence. But even here he figures as a forerunner. In 1925, before the basic works of Heidegger and Jaspers had come out, his article *Existence et Objectivité* had appeared in the *Revue de Métaphysique et de Morale*. In that article he stressed, in opposition to the idealists, the role of existence and of incarnation. Between 1915 and 1923 he wrote the second part of the *Journal Métaphysique*, in which he expounded the same views. He had developed the essential themes of his thought before becoming acquainted with the works of Heidegger, Jaspers and Kierkegaard. His thought, stimulated also by the work of Bergson, to which he owes a great deal, is, nevertheless, independent of them all. It is coincidence and not consanguinity that connects his philosophy with that of his contemporaries.

There is a very marked affinity between Marcel's thought and that of Jaspers. Both endeavoured, by a critical examination of objective knowledge, to save the idea of existence from being overpowered by the idea of Transcendence. Marcel and Jaspers were also able to point out numerous analogies between incarnation and limit-situations, between the *thou* and com-

concerned with the dehumanization of the modern world. Their train of thought and critical method are, in the last analysis, only the counterpart of the concrete ontology that is the essence of his entire philosophy.

munication, between secondary reflection and the reading of ciphers, between the two conceptions of the role of liberty. But the difference of rhythm and orientation between their two philosophies must also be noted. By putting the accent on choice, hindrance and frustration, the philosophy of Jaspers is one of liberty and paradox. Marcel's thought, which conceives liberty as power of adherence rather than power of choice, and puts the accent on participation, is a philosophy of being and mystery.[35]

That is why Marcel (like Heidegger, and for a like reason, too, despite their deep differences) does not welcome the label of existential philosophy. He even reproached Jaspers—perhaps too harshly—for the latter's "radical denial of the ontological as such".[36] And what is vastly more important, the appearance of Jean-Paul Sartre's *L'Être et le Néant* (1943) provoked him to denounce a philosophy that subordinates value to free choice. Indeed, his reaction against it tended to make him develop a metaphysic of essence and, in doing so, to fall back upon certain aspects of Platonism,[37] while still remaining faithful to his former insights. But even before that he had written: "A system of metaphysics built up in such a way that it leaves essences out of account or simply ignores them is liable to collapse like a house of cards".[38] Since then he has reiterated this assertion, but, this notwithstanding, he has refused to treat essence or value as a product of abstraction, an intelligible object. "Essence," he says, "is itself illuminating far more than it can be illuminated and *a fortiori* described. It is a nucleus. It is *the* nucleus, and it is only in so far as it is present to the con-

[35]See Paul Ricoeur, *Gabriel Marcel et Karl Jaspers, Philosophie du Mystère et Philosophies du Paradoxe*, Paris 1947.

[36]*Du Refus à l'Invocation*, 326.

[37]*Fontaine*, April 1946, 592; *Revue de Paris*, Sept. 1948, 135.

[38]*Du Refus à l'Invocation*, 152.

sciousness that the latter can itself be regarded as a source of illumination."[39]

In his preface to *Le Mystère de l'Être*, the author says he has written his book "not for an abstract or anonymous intelligence but for individual beings in order to rouse them to a deeper reflective life by a regular anamnesis, in the Socratic and Platonic sense of the word". He deliberately places his book under the aegis of Socrates and Plato, if only, says he, to protest "against those deplorable misunderstandings which his philosophy has had to put up with on account of that dreadful label 'existentialism'". Although he is loth to let his thought bear any label at all, if he were absolutely forced to choose one, he would resignedly opt for "neo-Socratism" or "Christian Socratism".[40] Such a title would assuredly "give a marvellously accurate idea of Marcel's mode of philosophizing: the free and agile spirit of Socrates operating within the framework of a philosophy of Christian inspiration".[41]

Every thinker has his limitations, and it sometimes happens that the deeper his insight into his own particular sphere, the more circumscribed is the area within which it is effective. Marcel rightly insists on the constant menace that confronts man in the modern world owing to the tendency of techological civilization to degrade man's person into a mere system of functions, and to deprive him of the sense of ontological mystery. In order that Marcel's criticism may be seen to be just, and that the high place accorded in his philosophy to the mystery of being may not run the risk of

[39]*Fontaine, loc. cit.*

[40]*Le Mystère de l'Être*, I, 5.

[41]Xavier Tillette, *Philosophes contemporains*, Paris 1962, 9, which includes an excellent essay on Marcel, complementary to ours. Marcel himself has given us a sketch of the genesis of the main theme of his philosophy in an article entitled *Vers une ontologie concrète* in *Encyclopédie Française*, XIX, 19, 14, 2–6.

appearing to be "reactionary", should they not be accompanied by some constructive thought on the nature of modern technology? History shows us that technology, too, has its advantages, and, in any case, there is no sense in sounding a retreat into the past. It is from our world as it exists today and from our own historical situation that we must go to meet the eternal.

Marcel does not hesitate to accuse modern society of worsening human relations by substituting a relationship based upon the third person (*l'on*) for the more intimate *thou* relationship of other days. From that he goes on to criticize democracy *qua* democracy and to exalt the personal virtues, the virtues of private life—friendship, love, fidelity. But if it is true that private life has more "ontological ballast" than social, political and economic life, must we not also be prepared to recognize the need for the bonds that unite us in society? Law and social institutions, the equality of men before the law, is it not their special function to protect the private life of the person? Surely it would have been wise for Marcel to have found room for some positive thought about their meaning and their function?

Finally, Marcel justly criticizes the degraded forms of intelligence and objective knowledge that have given birth to the various kinds of positivism. This criticism would be still more convincing if it were accompanied by a positive appreciation of objective and impersonal thought at its different levels, which would bring out, at the same time, by immanent reflection, its essential role and its limitations. Metaphysical thought itself, which ceases to have any hold on reality the moment it ceases to be related to existence and to participate in being, has recourse, however, to universal categories. Now, "secondary reflection" is sound only when dialectic and the experience of presence there encounter one another. Can a metaphysic of essence be worked out without uncovering the structure of this dialectic? We should like to have details of an epistemology of "undegraded" intelligence. We should then see that worship can, and ought to, be a mainstay for reflection and, moreover, that the movement that leads man to worship has an intelligible structure. Having so rightly stressed that proof of God must be established in God at the outset, Marcel might have analysed the dialectic of its movement. The fact that subjectivity plays a necessary part in it need not detract from its intellectual value. Indeed, the most recent scientific thought shows that this is happening already, to a certain extent, in the case of the general theories of physics and mathematics.[42]

Marcel's is a philosophy on the confines of philosophy. There lie its limitations. But there, also, lies its strength. However much we should like to see it brought into line, in some respects, with contemporary circumstances, far be it from us to deprive it of any of the merit of its great contribution to philosophical thought. Many owe to it their deliverance from a narrow rationalism or from nihilism. It has shown that love of creation can be linked with longing for the eternal, and the spirit of reflective criticism with the sense of mystery. For the non-believer in quest of truth, or the Christian who is a prey to doubt, it re-establishes that Christian or near-Christian climate of thought outside which faith can survive only with difficulty. To the theologians, also, Marcel's philosophy can also be a guide and a stimulant. In Marcel's own words, "such a philosophy is borne irresistibly towards a light, as yet faint and far away, but already quickening the heart of it, and soon to set it all aglow".[43]

[42]Our remarks here coincide with those of Paul Ricoeur in the work quoted in note 35 above, 161, 175–7, 300, 369.

[43]*Position* . . . 301.

VIII

PHILOSOPHY AND CHRISTIANITY IN THE
THOUGHT OF MAURICE BLONDEL

To approach Maurice Blondel's thought by examining the relationship between philosophy and Christianity is not to restrict ourselves to a marginal aspect, or a particular area, of his work; on the contrary it is to get at the very heart of it. Blondel has repeatedly said so himself at different times and in different terms: his primary and persistent intention has been to elaborate a philosophy which, in the course of its free and autonomous development, would spontaneously open towards Christianity. This was the purpose of his famous thesis *l'Action*, which appeared in 1893, and of numerous articles in defence, or in illustration, of it. And it was the purpose also of the immense philosophical testament of the period 1934 to 1946, which comprises, on the one hand, what the author calls his trilogy—*La Pensée, L'Être et les êtres*, and *l'Action* (second version)—and, on the other hand, *Philosophie et l'Esprit chrétien*. Throughout the entire corpus of his work, we find what is essentially the same intention—to construct a philosophy that, by the logic of its own rational movement, would progress naturally towards Christianity, and without actually going so far as to make the Christian faith imperative, would inevitably posit the Christian problem.

I have used the word "construct" deliberately. Blondel thought it was not enough to try and tack Christianity on to an existing philosophy that had arisen outside the sphere of Christian thought. He considered that no philosophy would be in accordance with the Gospel that did not, somehow, derive from the gospel, but he considered it essential, too, that any such philosophy should develop in an autonomous and rational manner. It seemed to him that no philosophy of this kind had yet come into being, and that it was his special mission in life to construct one.

It was a bold undertaking, and he never pretended it was anything but a difficult one. The link he wanted to forge between philosophy and Christianity would have, not only to respect but, to ensure the autonomy of the one and the transcendence of the other. Let us see how he set about it.

1. *The Encounter between Philosophy and Christianity*

The genesis of a train of thought will invariably shed some light on its significance. To begin with, then, let us take a look at the circumstances that led Blondel to conceive and to define his aim. He himself has explained these often enough in print—in what he has written personally and what has been written with his consent. We can learn still more about them from unpublished documents preserved in the Blondelian Archives in Aix-en-Provence, and from his private notebooks, some of which have been recently published.

These notebooks show that Blondel, from early youth, had a deeply-rooted Christian faith and an intense spiritual life. He strove earnestly to live up to that new birth spoken of in the gospel, and to observe that attitude of detachment from all things and from himself, which allows us to live in God and, then, purified in the process, to rediscover the love of all things. That life, which for him was the only true life, he fervently wished to communicate to those who did not know of it. He had the soul of an apostle.

This young man from the provinces who came up to the École Normale in 1881 had set his heart on sharing his spiritual insights with his fellow-students. Only too often, however, he ran his head against a wall. At the very idea of Christianity, a plea of demurrer was raised. One day, for example, he was met with the reply: "Why should I have to bother about something that happened nineteen hundred years ago in an obscure corner of the Roman Empire when I pride myself on my ignorance of so many really important events because they would narrow my whole mental outlook?"[1] We are not concerned here with the diversity of attitudes or convictions which the young student's faith encountered—dilettantism, scientism, critical philosophy, long-winded Spinozism and so on. What concerns us is that the violent clash of ideas and the shock that Blondel got from it, was the genesis of his philosophy. In order to make his unbelieving comrades understand that Christianity was of concern to them, he was compelled to enter as fully as he could into their spirit, all the while in pursuit of a truth they would never suspect was there. When he had recaptured it, he would reveal it to them and show them that it was the only truth that could lighten their darkness.

And so, the task that was to occupy Blondel for the rest of his days was first imposed on him in the shape of an antagonism, a conflict between modern thought and Catholicism, a conflict

[1]Quoted by Blondel in *Le Probleme de la philosophie catholique*, II, note.

that had to be found out in a dialogue on the terrain of man and of philosophy.

He has given us a particularly clear and accurate account of the nature of the conflict and of the conditions of the dialogue in the famous *Lettre* of 1896, commonly called *Lettre sur l'Apologétique*, an abridgement of an excessively long title which runs (in translation) "Letter on the Requirements of Contemporary Thought in the matter of Apologetics and on the use of Philosophical Method in the study of the Religious Problem".

> Modern thought is very quick to resent criticism that would impugn the notion of *immanence* as the indispensable pre-condition of philosophical thought. If there is one idea in the whole realm of modern thought which it cherishes as a definite step forward, it is the idea that nothing can get into a man's head that does not come out of it, in response, as it were, to a need to expand and develop, and that there is nothing in the nature of historical fact or traditional teaching, or obligation imposed from without, nothing in short that man will accept as truth and admit as precept, unless it is, in some way, autonomous and autochtonous. On the other hand, nothing is Christian and nothing is Catholic unless it is supernatural . . . supernatural in the strict sense of the word; that is to say, it is impossible for man to find out for himself, those (supernatural) things which, notwithstanding, it is sought to impose on his thought and on his will.[2]

The Christian supernatural, Blondel explains, confronts the philosopher with a twofold scandal. On the one hand, it is not

---

[2] *Lettre*, 34. (Page references are to the reprint in *Les Premiers Écrits de Maurice Blondel*, Paris 1956). There is an English trans. in A. Dru and I. Trethowan, *Maurice Blondel: Letter on Apologetics and History and Dogma*, London 1964.

authentic unless it is given from above and received. It is not something we discover, some offshoot of ourselves. On the other hand, this gratuitous, supernatural gift imposes on the receiver the obligation to accept it, so that, while we have no power to save ourselves, we have the power to plunge ourselves into eternal misery.[3]

But, adds the author, what appears to render these two sides of Christian revelation mutually incompatible, proves to be the very thing that provides the solution of the dilemma. If Christianity were optional, if it were permissible to refuse the divine gift offered to us, without bringing dire consequences upon ourselves, then our refusal to accept the call to higher, supernatural things would simply leave us at the human level, the level to which man can attain naturally, by his own un-aided efforts. In that case, the supernatural would present no philosophical problem at all. But if, on the other hand, the divine revelation regards any neutral or negative attitude on our part as a falling away, a positive and culpable lapse; if our refusal to accept the divine gift means that we contract a debt which only eternity can discharge, then, indeed, battle is joined, the difficulty is upon us, and the problem rears its head. For if it is true that the claims of divine revelation upon us are justified, it is no answer to say that we feel quite at home where we are, in our own human insufficiency; and this insufficiency, this impotence, this just, divine claim upon us, must all be reflected somehow in man's constitution and find an echo in even the most autonomous of philosophies.[4]

Blondel, of course, is here arguing hypothetically, *if* the claims of Christianity on us are justified, they *must* be reflected in every man's nature; the obligation imposed from *without* must be paralleled by the existence *within* of a need and the

[3]*Ibid.*, 35–6.
[4]*Ibid.*, 37.

urge to satisfy it and the expectation or the hope that it will be satisfied. If it is really necessary for man to accept the supernatural proclaimed by the Christian message, man's being must surely have some sign upon it to show that this is so. And, if the sign is there, then, man meditating upon man's being—that is, the philosopher philosophizing—will be able to discover it and to tell us what it is. And, by doing so, he will show that Christianity is of concern to every man.

That, precisely, is what Blondel set out to demonstrate. And his first step was to undertake a study of action.

This was to be his doctoral thesis: he had come to that decision while he was still at the École Normale. The subject was not accepted without demur; it was quite out of tune with the times. But that was the very reason why Blondel had chosen it. It struck him that a proper appreciation of the exigencies of action was what was most lacking among his fellow-students and in the philosophical circles in which he moved. All around him the prevalent attitude was that of the spectator, the detached onlooker. Dilettantism or aestheticism was then the fashion. The ideal of many intellectuals was to understand everything, to sample everything, to enjoy everything, without committing themselves to anything. As for the various trends of the current philosophies, Blondel thought they were too intellectual, too abstract, too far removed from concrete reality. In order to bring out once again the seriousness of life and, at the same time, re-establish contact with universal concrete reality, what could be better than a study of action? And what would offer more chances of finding, if it can be found at all, the point of insertion of Christianity in man—the point at which the first intimations of Christianity become apparent in man's make-up? For Christian life is essentially action: we make acts of faith and charity, we *practise* our religion.

But action, as Blondel envisages it, is not *praxis* in the Marxist sense; it is rather *praxis* in the Aristotelian sense. It is not the kind of action whereby man transforms nature and economic systems; it is the action whereby man fulfils his destiny through his activity in various spheres.

Noting that we act inevitably, Blondel asked himself whether it was possible to discover any meaning in man's action. "Has human life any meaning at all; has man a destiny, Yes or No?"[5] If there is a reply it must be wrapped up in our activity; it is there we must look for it. The philosopher, therefore, must place himself, so to speak, in the bosom of action itself, so as to share in the dialectic of real life and to try and discern the necessities inherent in every use of liberty. He must find out "what is inevitable and necessary in the total deployment of human action",[6] he must endeavour "to determine the chain of necessities that make up the drama of life and carry it on inexorably towards its *denouement*".[7] In short, he must discover the logic of action.

How was he to go about it? In order that the method should be rigorous, it would be best to presuppose nothing, to take nothing for granted—neither fact, nor principle, nor obligation. Men have conspired to invent a multiplicity of attitudes and doctrines in an endeavour to escape from the constraints that tradition seemed to want to burden them with. The philosopher, says Blondel, must become a conspirator *ad hoc* and join all these conspiracies if he wants to find out whether there is anything in them that justifies or condemns them. "The most stupid negations and the wildest extravagances of the human will must be probed to their roots to see if there is

[5]*L'Action* (1893), vii.
[6]*Ibid.*, 475.
[7]*Ibid.*, 473.

not one deep-seated, initial movement or impulse that persists always throughout them all, that is always cherished and craved, even when it is abjured or abused. Each of these various attitudes and doctrines must be probed for the principle that will enable judgement to be passed on it."[8]

Blondel then proceeds to examine the principal attitudes and doctrines that purport to confine human existence within specific limits. He shows how, in each case, the limits are inevitably overstepped by those who try, or pretend, to observe them. At every step, in fact, there is an evident disproportion between what man believes he is thinking and willing and what he thinks and wills in reality. There is always a discrepancy between the limits of the action and the movement of the will, between what is apparently willed (*la volonté voulue*) and what is basically willed (*la volonté voulante*). We are then shown that man can only fulfil himself by freely opening himself to action other than his own human action. And so, it appears that the human will is, at bottom, a longing for that gratuitous gift of God, a crying need of the supernatural. Christianity, concludes Blondel, seems to be the appropriate response to this.

Such, then, is the general plan of the bulky volume that came out in 1893 with the title (in English translation) "Action. An Attempt to formulate a critical Philosophy of Life and a Science of Practice". It is important to note, at the outset, that Blondel proceeds by reflection, and not by introspection. The *volonté voulante* he speaks of is not a conscious or subconscious will that can be discovered by careful introspection and compared with the *volonté voulue* as two projects are compared to see if they are compatible. The *volonté voulante* is at the core of every free attitude; it is the original, initial will

[8]*Ibid.*, xx.

that is necessarily implied by such an attitude. It is revealed only by reflection, and thus *indirectly*, as the condition that makes the *volonté voulue* possible at all. The latter alone is an object of *direct* knowledge. A disharmony between the two wills must be understood as a contradiction within the *volonté voulue* itself.

When Blondel, therefore, believes he has discovered in the heart of the human will a need of, a longing for, the supernatural, let us not suppose he invites us to think of it as a need or longing plainly present in our consciousness. On the contrary, when addressing himself to the non-believer, he assumes that this need or longing is not experienced by such a person. But, by rational and rigorous argument, he wants to make us see that such a need is *implied* in human action, and that this is evident even in the act which rejects the supernatural.

Finally, if such terms as need, expectation, longing, seem vague and, perhaps, susceptible of misinterpretation, Blondel's other terms such as idea, notion, necessity are definite enough. In any case, it becomes obvious immediately that there is no question here of verifying a state of consciousness but of getting to understand the internal logic of action.

2. *Genesis of the Idea of the Supernatural*

We have seen now what caused Blondel to conceive his philosophic plan, how he defined it, and the method he thought best to adopt in carrying it out.

How is the plan worked out in the structure of *l'Action*? Let us run through that work quickly and endeavour to grasp how the internal logic of human action gives rise to the idea of the supernatural, how this idea is shown to be necessary to man, and how it leads the human mind towards Christianity.

The author proceeds by stages. It is important to distinguish these stages carefully. If the distinctive character of each is not kept well in mind, there is a risk that Blondel's argument, at some stage, may appear to us as a confused magma in which philosophy loses its rational purity and Christianity its transcendence—which would, of course, be absolutely contrary to his intention.

The first two parts of the book need not detain us. From our point of view they are merely preliminary. The author first establishes, by a critical survey of the dilettantism then in vogue, that the problem of destiny cannot be burked, and that nothing posits it more perfectly than the very act that is designed to suppress it. Blondel then shows, by directing his critical apparatus on pessimism, that a negative solution is untenable: to will nothing is a contradiction in terms, for to will at all must be to will something.

Starting from this first affirmation, which we can take as both necessary and obvious, Blondel goes on to review in succession the different spheres of human activity, justifying each by the impossibility of doing without it, and overstepping each by the impossibility of limiting oneself to it. This forms the subject of the third part of the work, which is entitled "The phenomenon of action".

The author begins with the most elementary datum—sensation. He shows that it suffers from an insufficiency that man remedies by creating science. Science, in turn, implies synthetic activity, the constituent action of a subject. From awareness of this, liberty must necessarily emerge. In order to live and grow, liberty must be deployed and incarnated in action, and in grappling with the resistance of the body and of the world it builds up individuality. The individual, in turn, seeks and secures outside himself, a complement to himself: he wants to found a social group. In this way, the human will begets family, fatherland, humanity. Man's will extends to higher things: it creates metaphysics and a moral code that implies the absolute of duty. And so, the final goal towards which free and conscious action is seen to aspire is an absolute.

But, lo and behold! man, in an attempt to put the final touch to himself and become self-sufficing, tries to appropriate and absorb the infinite and the absolute by placing it in, by "thinking it into", an object accessible to him, if only in thought. Here we have the phenomenon of superstition. Blondel discovers it in the worship of science or of art, in pseudo-mysticisms, and even in rationalistic theism and moralism. This attitude of superstition, he says, implies a contradiction. It consists, in effect, in making something more of such-and-such a phenomenon than it really is. We have seen how no such phenomenon satisfies the aspirations of the will. Yet, under the influence of superstition, man loses all inclination to look elsewhere for an object to attach himself to everlastingly. "All these attempts lead to this doubly imperative conclusion: it is impossible not to recognize the insufficiency of the whole natural order and not to feel a fundamental lack and longing within oneself; it is impossible to find within oneself the wherewithal to satisfy this religious requirement, which is *necessary* but *impracticable*. There, put baldly, are the conclusions of the determinism (i.e., the dialectic) of human action."[9]

The last passage calls for some little comment. It marks, as a matter of fact, the first stage in the genesis of the idea of the supernatural. The word "supernatural" does not, and could not, appear in it, for it is assumed that the idea of God has not emerged in the dialectic at this stage, and the term that qualifies divine action, therefore, cannot be used. Blondel simply points out that the determinism (i.e., the dialectic) of action leads us to recognize the insufficiency of the natural order. By natural

[9]*Ibid.*, 319.

order he does not mean, as theologians often take it to mean, the world envisaged in its relation to the Creator. On the contrary, he abstracts from this relation and applies the term "natural order" to the whole field of human activity. In short, he confines himself, for the time being, to stating the result of his inquiry in language that steers clear of the specific as far as possible. And this result, to all appearance wholly negative, is that the *necessary* condition for the completion of human action is *inaccessible* to human action.

This dialectic of the "inaccessible necessary" dominates the remainder of the book. It brings out the idea of God, thereby confronting man with the supreme option of his life, his real "moment of truth". The idea of the supernatural now makes its appearance, but in a form as yet undetermined. This second stage of its genesis is discussed in the fourth part of the book, which is called "The necessary nature of action". Let us now see how Blondel's dialectic proceeds in practice.

The fact that man looks for the key to his self-sufficiency in the natural order and fails to find it, brings him face to face with a crisis. This state of affairs is not only apparent in all his activities; it is immanent in the human condition itself. Man wills, certainly, but he has not willed to will; in what he wills, he everywhere encounters obstruction and distress; in what he does, incurable weaknesses crop up as a matter of course, with faults whose consequences it is beyond him to repair. And, at last, death puts an end to his activities for good and all. On the other hand, this seeming frustration of willed action brings out the indestructibility of voluntary action, of man's power of willing, for I should not have been conscious of this frustration if there had not been a will within me that could rise superior to life's contradictions. This, then, is my plight: I cannot escape from the necessity of willing myself, and yet it is impossible for me to catch up with myself and make certain of myself, directly, by any effort of my own. I can neither stop, nor draw back, nor go forward, by myself. What will be the outcome of this crisis, this internal conflict?

"It is this conflict," Blondel continues, "that explains why there must need be present in man's consciousness a new affirmation; and, indeed, it is the reality of this 'necessary presence' that makes us conscious of the conflict. There is 'one thing necessary'. The whole movement of the determinism, of the dialectic, is towards that 'one thing necessary', towards that end which is also a source, the source from which springs the very dialectic whose whole purpose is to bring us back to it."[10]

Sustained by this robust dialectic of action, proofs of God's existence acquire fresh vigour. They reveal the presence of God at the very centre of our existence, in our contact with things, through the plenitude that these things offer us, as well as through the intrinsic indigence of the things themselves.

The thought of God, Blondel continues, which is necessarily born of the dynamism of our interior life, also necessarily has an effect upon it. The thought of God impresses the stamp of transcendence upon our action. We want to possess this God who is present to us; we want in some way to become him. Now, he is, beyond all question, something we can neither reach nor possess by our own efforts. And so we are faced with a decisive choice, a choice that will decide the meaning that life shall have for us from now on. "Is man willing to give ungrudging consent to his supersession by God for the rest of his life, even if, so to speak, it should be the death of him? Or will he go on trying to be self-sufficing, taking no account of God, availing of God's necessary presence but not willing it, borrowing from God the strength to do without God, willing

[10]*Ibid*, 339.

infinitely without willing the infinite?"[11] Blondel is aware that the dilemma does not present itself to everybody in as clear-cut and close-knit a way as that. But, he says, if the thought that there is something to be made of life presents itself to every mind, surely then, in some shape or form, more or less clearly, more or less obscurely, the call must come to everybody to solve the capital problem of "the one thing necessary"?

Here we are at the centre of gravity of Blondel's philosophy. Lest anyone should have failed to recognize it even in the foregoing passage, he repeats it at the end of his book. "The heart of the matter," he says, "lies entirely in this necessary conflict that arises within the human will and imposes on it a choice between two inevitable alternatives, a choice by which man prefers to remain his own master, uncommitted to anything outside himself, or surrenders himself to the divine command of which he has become more or less vaguely conscious."[12]

We must note that Blondel is not speaking here as a Christian addressing Christians. His words are meant for everybody, even for those who are ignorant of Christianity, in the hope that, by means of his philosophy, he can show them the logic that governs all human life. Blondel wants to help each of us to discover in himself the truth that passes judgement on him, and the insufficiency he must acknowledge in order to complete and achieve himself.

Proceeding on the same lines, he works out the inevitable consequences of each of the two possible options. If man thinks he can be self-sufficing without God, by restricting his ambition to the field of his activity, he belies his indestructible will. That means the death of action. But how is he to set about

[11]*Ibid.*, 354–5.
[12]*Ibid.*, 487.

throwing himself open to the action of God? Let him act in all things with detachment. Let him accept the suffering and the sacrifices demanded of him. And let him consider everything he does as the gift of God, as if he himself had no part in it.

This third point is especially important to us here, because it is through it that the author comes to mention the supernatural. Man ultimately tends to recognize, Blondel explains, that he cannot achieve his necessary end by his own efforts. *"Absolutely impossible and absolutely necessary to man, that is what the notion of the supernatural really means:* man's action transcends man; and the purpose of all his reasoning power is to see that he cannot—must not—be satisfied with that."[13]

Here, certainly, is one of the passages that have caused most embarrassment to sympathetic readers, theologians, and even philosophers. To want to establish the absolute necessity of the supernatural by an analysis of action, surely this is contrary to the Christian dogma that says the divine gift is freely given? And surely, too, this oversteps the limits of rational thought? We must admit that this passage of Blondel's would be difficult to defend, if we had to take his use of the word supernatural here to mean the gift that God has made of himself to man, in Jesus Christ. But that interpretation would be completely wrong; it would only show that sufficient notice had not been taken of the fact that Blondel, in determining the genesis of the idea of the supernatural, proceeds by stages, that he is here at the end of the second stage, that he has not yet expressly introduced—as he will do at the beginning of the third stage— the idea of Christianity; he is keeping to a more general idea and avoiding the positive and the particular.

All he wants to say at the moment is simply this: "Our role is to ensure that God is wholly in us as he is in himself,

---

[13] *Ibid.*, 388. The italics are ours.

and to recognize his efficacious presence in the very principle of our consent to his sovereign action".[14] (This passage is taken out of its immediate context, but many others could be quoted to the same effect.) In other words, it is necessary that, in his thought and in his conduct, man, the spiritual creature, shall freely recognize his inevitable dependence with regard to the Creator: man can only enter into communion with God through God's initiative and sovereign action. This sovereign action of God is what is "absolutely impossible and absolutely necessary to man"; it is that to which the term supernatural is applied here.

To speak of *absolute* necessity in such a context is not merely permissible; it is rendered necessary by the essential relation of the creature to his Creator. Suppose the Christian revelation was non-existent or unknown, but man, nevertheless, desired to enter into communion with God. He would have to recognize that such communion (whatever its form) is only possible through the initiative and action of God.

Rightly or wrongly, Blondel thinks he has found an adumbration of this idea in Aristotle. Having brought out man's inability to achieve his necessary end solely by his own efforts, he goes on to say: "Aristotle had a presentiment of this when he said, 'There is in man a better life than that of man, and man is not capable of keeping up that better life; it must be that man has something of the divine dwelling within him'."[15] This passage immediately precedes that which mentions the absolute necessity of the supernatural. Given that the author has certainly not attributed to Aristotle an explicit knowledge of the Christian supernatural, it is clear that here again he does not envisage the supernatural in its specifically Christian form.

[14]*Ibid.*, 387.
[15]*L'Action*, 388.

What Blondel sees developing from the dialectic of human action is the idea of a supernatural as yet undetermined, that is to say, an idea of the Infinite and the Absolute that every man vaguely desires, knowing that it is not his to be had for the taking. This idea must arise, in one form or another, in every human being, even in those ignorant of Christianity. It is man's toothing stone, the point at which the Christian supernatural is inserted in him. It constitutes, so to speak, the *a priori* thanks to which he will be able to recognize and accept it.

We now come to the fifth, and last, part of *l'Action*, which is headed "The consummation of action". It marks the third stage in the genesis of the idea of the supernatural. Here the notion of the specifically Christian supernatural makes its appearance. We can see it taking shape in the very first pages; the supernatural order whose necessity he will henceforth demonstrate will be that "which, from outside, proposes dogmas for our belief".[16] Particular attention must be paid to the words "from outside". Here the philosopher no longer relies on his own resources for the idea of the supernatural; he takes up the idea of the supernatural put forward by Christianity, and considers it.

What is his justification for doing so, in view of the fact that the Christian idea originated outside the domain of philosophy? The answer is, because the idea of the supernatural that he has found to be present in every individual is as yet undetermined, and he must find a way to make it determinate and definitive. Blondel then goes on to consider whether the Christian notion of the supernatural would not adequately fulfil this purpose. In other words, he proceeds to ask himself whether historical Christianity, with its dogmas and practices,

[16]*Ibid.*, 391.

would not be the deciding factor in man's relation to the Absolute, whether it would not be the definitive solution to his problem.

He is not at all concerned to reconstruct the corpus of Christian doctrine on a rational basis; that would be to contradict the very idea he had in mind. Indeed, according to Christian doctrine it would be illegitimate "to pretend to discover by reason alone what the content of revelation must be in order that it may be recognized as knowledge".[17] But Blondel thinks that the philosopher has the right to *confront* Christian teaching with human aspirations. He explains why this is so. "It is legitimate," he writes, "to push research as far as the point at which we feel we ought to desire intensely something analogous to what these outside dogmas lay before us. It is legitimate to consider these dogmas, in the first instance, as not indubitably revealed, but as revealing; that is to say, to confront them with the profound aspirations of the will and to discover in them, if it is to be found, the reflection of our real wants and the longed-for answer that will satisfy us. It is legitimate to accept them as hypotheses, like the geometricians, when they assume that a certain hypothesis will solve a problem, and then proceed to verify this assumption by means of analysis."[18]

This passage furnishes the best illustration of Blondel's procedure in this third stage of his demonstration. To follow it, a person need not admit the truth of Christian dogma; the dogma is considered simply as a hypothesis. In other words, the existence or reality of the Christian supernatural order is placed in parenthesis; the idea alone is retained for consideration. And this idea is utilized as an ultimate indicator of the

[17]*Ibid.*, 391.

[18]*Ibid.*, 391.

aspirations of the will, or as a sort of cipher-stencil (*grille*) that will enable us to decipher our wants. If the attempt succeeds, if it appears that acceptance of the supernatural is the indispensable condition of the consummation of human action, then the idea envisaged at the outset as a hypothesis, will thereafter appear as a necessary hypothesis.

Blondel then shows how the idea of revelation and the various characteristics of Christian revelation, the necessity of faith and of religious practice, seem, in some way, called for by the dialectic of human action. In fact, "there is an infinite present in all our willed actions, and we cannot of ourselves retain that infinite in our thoughts or reproduce it by our human effort".[19] From this arise the ideas of revelation, the mediation of salvation, faith, and sacramental practice.

In carrying out this demonstration, the author simply deploys an entirely logical sequence, a series of completely formal relations. He does not pronounce upon the truth of the dogma, upon the reality of the supernatural, proclaimed by Christianity. To affirm that reality, he says, is the concern not of philosophy but of faith. Only through the experience of faith can man, enlightened by the divine light, discern the reality of the divine gift. Philosophy is an invitation to attempt that experience but is no substitute for it; it stops short at the threshold.

Let us now take a backward glance at the way over which we have travelled. In the first place, Blondel, we see, has established the insufficiency of the natural order; he has shown that the *indispensable* condition for the consummation of human action is *inaccessible* to human action. This dialectic of the indispensable inaccessible governs and shapes all the subsequent course of the argument. Blondel is always at pains

---

[19]*Ibid.*, 418.

to point out that the demands of the will exceed its power to
satisfy them. Out of this the idea of the necessity of the supernatural emerges, in two stages. In the first, the necessity is
absolute, but the supernatural is not positively determined. In
the second, the necessity is hypothetical, but the hypothesis
on which it is based is the Christian supernatural order. What
appears in the first stage is the absolute necessity of throwing
oneself open to God's action, whatever it may be. What
appears in the second, is the necessity to accept God's positive
revelation, if it is manifested to the subject through the medium
of the Christian religion. The one invites us to a sort of faith,
or openness, of the reason, a generosity of heart; the other
invites us to theological faith.

Let us not imagine, however, that Blondel superposes one
stage of the supernatural upon the other. The second idea of the
supernatural is merely a subsequent determination of the first.
The philosopher can only arrive at the formal meaning of the
Christian notion by continually referring it to the undetermined idea which is to be found in all human beings,
even those outside the Christian fold. That is why Blondel
could write: "Philosophy only considers the supernatural in
so far as the idea of it is immanent in us".[20]

We can now see how the author of *l'Action* resolves the
problem set by the encounter between modern philosophy
and Christianity. It will be recalled that, in face of the demands
Christianity makes upon us, demands that seem to run counter
to the very principle of modern philosophy, Blondel had
reasoned thus: if it is true that the acceptance of the Christian
supernatural is obligatory upon us under pain of everlasting
perdition, there must be in man a trace, and in philosophy an
echo, of the Christian claim on man. We have to thank

[20]*Lettre*, 86–7.

Blondel for bringing to light that trace and that echo; they are, indeed, the very logic of action. For the logic that invites man to deploy his activity in the worldly field, also causes him to throw himself open to the gift of a higher life, or, if he retreats into his insufficient self, to pronounce sentence of condemnation on himself. Blondel's philosophy paves the way for the Christian faith, because it discloses that the internal logic of human action is, fundamentally, identical with the internal logic of Christianity.

3. *Blondel's thought accords with Christian dogma and the require-*
   ments of reason

We can see the care Blondel took, throughout his work, to ensure both the rational autonomy of his philosophic argument and the transcendence of the Christian supernatural. Has he really succeeded? Many have thought so; others have had grave doubts. The author of *l'Action* has often had to explain, justify, and reinforce his argument.

This is not the place, however, for a detailed discussion of the opposition his views have aroused in some quarters. I will confine myself to a few brief observations.

The objection raised by a number of theologians can be summed up as follows: if it can be established by purely human reasoning that the supernatural is necessary to man, then the supernatural becomes natural and is no longer a free gift of God to man. This is an understandable, but unduly hasty, objection. To my mind, it should quickly disappear as soon as Blondel's intention and the progressive development of his thought are fully grasped.

1. If Blondel undertakes to demonstrate, by philosophical argument, the need or the necessity of the supernatural, he does so in order that the demands made upon man by Christianity may be taken seriously. The object of his demonstration,

therefore, is to establish, not that *God ought* to give himself to man because, if he does not, he leaves man, his creature, unsatisfied, but that *man ought* to accept the free gift proclaimed by the Christian message. The demonstration does not require that God shall reveal himself; it simply brings to light the *a priori*—the internal dispositions—thanks to which man is enabled to perceive and accept the claims of divine revelation.

2. Blondel's dialectic always aims at making the supernatural appear "indispensable as well as inaccessible to man".[21] The second of these characteristics is as essential as the first. "The supernatural," he says, "will conform to the idea we have of it only in so far as we admit it is out of our human reach."[22] Which means to say that the supernatural connotes to the philosopher something inaccessible to human effort.

3. We have seen that the idea first occurs to the philosopher in an undetermined form, and that, in order to determine it, he confronts it with the Christian dogmas, considered as hypotheses. By adopting this procedure, he makes us recognize that the content of revelation cannot originate in our own general consciousness; it comes from outside and has a historical origin. There is still room for the free action of God in history.

4. Finally, in establishing that the science of action is not a substitute for action, Blondel makes us understand that only the experience of faith can discern in the Christian message the gift of God in all its freshness and overwhelming liberality.

These brief observations suffice to indicate how the author of *l'Action* has succeeded in revealing an immanent desire in man for the supernatural, without bringing the supernatural

[21]*Ibid.*, 43.

[22]*Ibid.*, 41.

order into the (purely natural and rational) dialectic of human action.

Blondel has also been taken to task by a number of philosophers who contend that, inasmuch as it pretends to establish the necessity of adherence to the Christian supernatural, his thought derogates from the laws of rational argument; it presupposes, they say, what it professes to establish; it is an apologetic and not a philosophy.

Blondel always protested against this accusation. He frankly admitted that his thought stemmed from the Christian idea, had been developed on the hypothesis that Christianity is true, and owed much to study of the New Testament and the works of St Bernard and other spiritual authors. But, when he argued as a philosopher, the only parts of Christian doctrine he made use of were those that he considered were capable of rational justification.

In the course of his philosophical argument, he never presupposes the truth of Christianity or even the presence in man of a will for the infinite. From the outset, he suspends his profession of faith and rules out every postulate. And he proceeds by an indirect and negative method. He enters successively into the spirit of all the attitudes and all the doctrines that dismiss the idea of the supernatural. He even casts a cold eye on the idea himself. And it is only when forced to do so by rational necessity that he moves forward from each negative position. He discovers, in fact, that every negation includes the very idea it purports to deny.

Neither at the beginning nor at the end of his argument does Blondel actually affirm the truth of Christianity. He certainly makes no secret of his desire to orient minds towards the Christian faith. But he knew that faith could never be the conclusion of any philosophy, for faith is a free act and a God-given gift. The philosopher comes to a stop at the threshold of faith and refrains from saying the one little word that would reveal him to be a believer.

We see, then, that although Blondel's philosophy is developed on the hypothesis of the truth of Christianity, it does not begin by presupposing that truth. Although it aims at preparing minds to receive the faith, it never crosses the threshold of the faith. From start to finish, it deliberately remains entirely within the realm of pure reason. The reader, of course, may not be convinced by the author's demonstration; he may even fancy he detects faults in the author's logic. That is one of the hazards to which all philosophies are subject. But that does not justify criticism which would impugn the intellectual autonomy of the author's thought and its fidelity to the principles that govern all philosophy.

Our main object in all that we have said was to show how Blondel's philosophy is oriented towards the Christian idea and, therefore, induces minds to give serious consideration to that idea.[23] The reader may have noted that, to attain its end, it surveys the whole range of human activity and justifies that

[23] We have developed the same theme, at much greater length, in our work, *Blondel et le christianisme*, Paris 1961. In an article in *Critique* (Feb. 1962) and in a paper reprinted in the collection *Centenaire de Maurice Blondel* (101–32) and entitled *Intention philosophique de Maurice Blondel*, M. Jean Lacroix was good enough to speak favourably of our work and we thank him warmly for it. We are glad to see he agrees with our view as regards the meaning of the first (1893) version of *l'Action*. As to the relation between that work and the trilogy, we are glad to say also that our interpretation differs much less from his own than he seems to think; the point on which we differ is not "radical"; it is implied in the intention underlying all Blondel's works and consistently maintained by him. Besides, if his last works strike us as less satisfying than *l'Action* as regards the relation of philosophy to Christianity, it is not because our perspective was more theological than philosophical. On the contrary it was precisely because we viewed the matter in a philosophic light, that we expressed our embarrassment at Blondel's attempt to insert theological concepts into his philosophical argument in the Trilogy (Df. our work quoted above, 126–8).

activity in each of its elements. Welcoming everything that is of interest to mankind, Blondel's philosophy aspires to be an integral philosophy. Its integrality would be more obvious if we had been able to examine the trilogy also; before embarking on a study of human action, it considers human thought, being, and action in general. Together with *La Philosophie et l'Esprit chrétien*, which is its complement, it would give us more material for our main theme. However, rather than disperse the reader's attention over several of Blondel's works, we thought it better here to focus it on the work that is a real breakthrough in the history of philosophy and remains the author's masterpiece—*l'Action* of 1893.[24]

Is it too much to hope that what we have said will induce our readers to go back to that masterpiece? Blondel's philosophy, of course, like that of his contemporaries, has now an old-fashioned look. But surely we must have been struck by the fact that the philosophy of action heralded the existential philosophies well in advance? In any case, a vigorous and well-grounded philosophy that has so well handled an essential and persistent human problem can never die. Even in a world so greatly changed from Blondel's day, and in an intellectual climate so utterly different, his philosophy cannot sound entirely strange. In what concerns the meaning of human life, and particularly the relation of thought or action to the demands and promises of Christianity, Blondel has shown so much understanding of the crucial point that he can still shed some light on our own situation.

[24]We have taken a more general view in a paper entitled *La Pensée de Maurice Blondel* read at the *Académie des Sciences morales et politiques* on 19 Feb. 1962. See the *Revue des Travaux de l'Académie des Sciences morales et politiques*, 1962, 1. semestre, 88–102.